The Modern Practical Approach
to Teaching English

Thomas A. Lund

THE MODERN PRACTICAL APPROACH TO TEACHING ENGLISH

Parker Publishing Company, Inc.
West Nyack, New York

PRINTED IN THE UNITED STATES OF AMERICA
ISBN 0-13-596106-8
B & P

*To Rene and Judy and Cliff
who put up with me then,
and Jo who puts up with me now.*

The Practical Value of This Book . . . .

Before I entered the field of education, and during my early years of radio announcing and programing, my amazement never ceased at the low premium the industry seemed to place on effective communications—particularly with respect to its trite, unimaginative, verbose commercial copy; double, triple, and even quadruple spot announcements between program segments; "commercial" pollution of the programs themselves; and prosaic, overdone program formats. I know now that the industry was not totally at fault. It is simply that our society does not produce very many good communicators. More than a decade of experience as an educator has taught me at least one of the reasons why: In large measure, we educators are not teaching *all* of the language.

This book explores the special problems which have created this state of affairs and offers some modern, practical ways in which you as an English teacher can solve them.

One big problem is the English curriculum guide. Another is heavy enrollment and oversized classes. Still another is education's apparent obsession with trivia at the expense of essentials. We can't, of course, abolish the curriculum guide, but we can transcend it. Large classes I suppose are here to stay, but there are ways to make them less cumbersome. Trivia need never be, but education is a bureaucracy and bureaucracy breeds trivia, seldom recognizing it for what it is. Happily, where the bureaucracy fails, the teacher can step in, as indeed he must, and greatly reduce if not eliminate trivia.

The most serious problem of all, however, is our failure to recognize language for what it is—a means to the most noble goal in education—effective communications.

Given a roomful of students, subject matter, and a teacher, we have the ingredients for a happening. The latent force of a meaningful interchange of ideas is present and needs only a catalyst (you) to set it in motion. In the English classroom, this force is by definition closer to the surface than in any other academic environment because *it is co-identical with the subject matter.* The English classroom is *the* marketplace for idea exchange—or at least it should be.

This book is for those teachers who realize that curriculum guides often do not really guide, and who search for practices in education that will serve to reduce the burden of large classes. It is written primarily for junior and senior high school teachers, but there is something of value in it for teachers at every level of education. Its objectives certainly suggest as much. They are three in number: first, to lay bare some of the problems common to all of us in education; second, to present some realistic and practical solutions to them; and third, to describe in detail a language program which takes full advantage of the opportunities that recognition and resolution of these problems can make possible.

You are not unfamiliar with the problems which will be described in this book, but it is quite possible you may not have hit upon ways to solve some of them. In this respect, I think, the book has real significance for you, whether you are teaching at the elementary or secondary level. As for the language program it describes, its techniques and characteristics are applicable specifically to secondary education; however, in general terms, it can be applied to any language program at whatever level of education.

The book is the result of 13 years of teaching experience. It offers no gimmicks which promise instant success, just realistic solutions to real problems. It is based on realities—the reality of curriculum, the reality of heavy classloads, and the reality of a society plagued by the petty.

During my 13 years of teaching, I have learned the importance of *listening to my students* and the need to separate the relevant from the irrelevant. It is the irrelevant in language teaching that has blunted our efforts—students and teachers alike—the irrelevance of grammar and the study of literature without consistent practice in oral and written language manipulation; the irrelevance of language drill with unrelated and often banal sentences; the irrelevance of a talking teacher who all too often has nothing to say; and the irrelevance of the mute student who as often as not has a great deal to say.

Admittedly, the adolescent has the reputation of being a notoriously vocal animal, but there are outlets for vocality other than the mouth, and idea exchange is not necessarily synonymous with noise. Most of my students, I like to think, cherish the one day every other week during which they spend the period silently enjoying the paperback of their choice in the complete absence of a vocal teacher. And while they manifest some dismay (I suspect, insincere) over the fact that we spend only 15 minutes a week on language analysis, they are content to leave it at that and enter into the quieter world of creative writing for the rest of the period and remain there for another 55 minutes the following day. We do resemble a legislative body on frequent occasions, occasions more formal or less formal, according to circumstances. But however we communicate with one another, it is understood we have freedom of speech—qualified only by the admonition to "keep it clean."

I presume, then, to describe actual experiences that offer

practical ways of making your classroom what every English classroom must be if it is to be at all—a meaningful happening. The fact that frequently it is anything but, is a sad commentary when one considers we are dealing here with what has rightly been called "the supreme event in human existence"—language.

THOMAS A. LUND

ACKNOWLEDGMENT

*My thanks to
SU TENNES
for the use of
her excellent
materials
center.*

Contents

The Practical Value of This Book **7**

Chapter 1 – THE ENGLISH TEACHER'S QUANDARY: A
WAY OUT **17**
*Problems: The guide, heavy enrollments,
trivia. . . . Descriptive analysis of their
seriousness. . . . How teachers compound their predicament. . . . Solutions: Transcend the guide; adopt
staggered schedule; decrease length and
number of tests; eliminate grading and
other busywork whenever possible. . . .
Summary.*

Chapter 2 – TEACHING WRITING IN A MODERN
LABORATORY ATMOSPHERE **40**
*Composition—the orphan of language
teaching. . . . Some reasons why. . . .
Techniques: A year-long writing unit.
. . . Begin by teaching fundamentals of
paragraph writing. . . . Revise writing
unit regularly. . . . Teach syntax through
writing. . . . Advance to multipara-
graph writing. . . . Emphasize dialogue
credibility. . . . Expand on your writing
base with an eclectic approach. . . .
Teaching poetry: What you can expect
from your students. . . . Haiku. . . .
Revision techniques: A handy formula.
. . .Your role. . . . Summary.*

Chapter 3 – ORGANIZING AND IMPLEMENTING AN
EFFECTIVE ORAL COMPOSITION PROGRAM   **78**
*"Speech" complements writing. . . .
Give it major stress. . . . You and your
students need it. . . . Oral composition
adapts well to the staggered academic
schedule. . . . Techniques: Use evaluating device. . . . Specific remedies for
oratorical faults. . . . Make students
work with card notes. . . . Use of evaluating sheet is effective. . . . Student-
orient your program. . . . Select provocative subject matter. . . . Limit discussion time. . . . The round-robin resource
unit. . . . Summary.*

Chapter 4 – BALANCING YOUR COURSE WITH A
SENSIBLE APPROACH TO GRAMMAR   . **102**
*About intuitive grammar. . . . Tech-
niques: Eliminate text. . . . Use your
own outline of syntax. . . . Study syntax
from student writing. . . . Give short
programed learning tests. . . . Evidence
of grammar's nonrelationship to language
skills. . . . Summary.*

Chapter 5 – ALTERNATIVES IN THE
TEACHING OF VOCABULARY   .   . **119**
*De-emphasize the workbook. . . . Em-
phasize word-meaning. . . . Techinques:
Give workbook exercises optional status.
. . . Vocabulary and programed learning.
. . . Alternate between the spelling-
meaning test and the spelling-only test.
. . . Make spelling fun. . . . Use inter-
student correcting when possible. . . .
Keep drillwork minimal. . . . Summary.*

Chapter 6 – ESTABLISHING A DIVERSIFIED
READING LAB **137**
*Techniques: Make your own develop-
mental reading lab for problem readers.*

*. . . Motivate readers with paperbacks.
. . . Build your classroom library
through membership in one or more paperback book clubs. . . . Group reading.
. . . Teach average and above-average
readers the novel, poetic devices through
poetry survey and end your survey with a
major work. . . . The junior high school
survey. . . . The senior high school survey. . . . Short discussions of literature
selections are realistic and effective. . . .
Teaching the novel. . . . Teaching conventional developmental reading. . . .
Give students free-reading days regularly.
. . . Summary.*

Chapter 7 – THE VALUE OF WRITTEN STUDENT
COURSE EVALUATIONS 168
*Student opinion through course evalua-
tions has value for you. . . . The student
view of education. . . . Constructive criticism sometimes helps. . . . About that
grammar. . . . Positive comments build
your ego, if nothing else. . . . Students
sometimes suggest valid alternatives for
your teaching program. . . . Their opinions are often entertaining. . . . Summary.*

Chapter 8 – SPARKING STUDENTS TO THEIR TOP
CREATIVE LEVELS 180
*Creativity—one point of view. . . . Sam-
ple products: The single-paragraph composition. . . . The multi-paragraph composition. . . . Narrative with dialogue.
. . . Poetry. . . . Haiku.*

INDEX 219

1

The English Teacher's Quandary: A Way Out

You, today's English teacher, carry on your shoulders an awesome responsibility. To you has been given the task of helping to develop in the youth of the nation, skills without which their education would be impossible, and their ability to communicate as they mature, something less than adequate. The responsibility is not only awesome; it might literally be termed herculean. For on the road to its fulfillment you are being stalked by a twentieth-century, man-made hydra. It shadows you furtively as you go about your work as an educator. It follows you into your classroom. It sits with you in your office when your teaching day is through. It is a cunning beast, mute, all but invisible, yet able by its mere presence to influence your every action as a teacher. It is a seeker of power, a seducer, a dissembler. It enfeebles, beguiles, suggests expediency when solution is needed. It is a crisis-maker.

What is this monster? We shall name it Oblivia, for reasons which will presently be made clear. In one sense, it is less formidable than the beast which confronted our mythological hero: Your hydra is only three-headed. But, alas, unlike our hero, you can resort to decapitation of none of its three heads; you must coexist with all of them. They are the *curriculum guide, oversized classes,* and *trivia*—not necessarily in the order of their virulence. No *myth,* your monster.

The English Curriculum Guide: Dissembler

Work on committees, attendance at summer institutes, and involvement in graduate work over a period of 13 years has made me reasonably familiar with English curriculum guides and their eccentricities, and in all that time I have never run across one which stipulates in its composition section, specifically, how often students should be allowed to engage in creative written and oral expression. What's more, most of the guides I have seen are vague about the sequence and scope of their composition programs. Hardly less disturbing is the fact that English curriculum guides are so frighteningly similar in their language. Virtually all of them embark on dreamy, pedantic, and seemingly interminable journeys in such public-relations jargon as ". . . to appreciate literary beauty and the force of style . . . to develop admiration for desirable qualities in literary characters . . . to learn the structural tendencies of the English sentence . . . to augment vocabulary commensurate with the other language skills . . ."; ad infinitum. All of which I suppose are legitimate aims in any language course. But must curriculum guides, especially English curriculum guides, read like "chamber of commerce" rhetoric? Could we say, for instance, "We are teaching literature so that students may come to realize that reading can be downright enjoyable, informative, and self-developing? . . . language analysis to satisfy a curiosity as to why the English sentence comes out the way it does? . . . vocabulary because it is the stuff of language? . . . composition because it represents the crucial half of a two-dimensional thing called communications?" Can't curriculum guides, at least the language arts sections, reflect what education is really all about —*clear, concise communications?*

Now, perhaps English teachers *can* or even *want* to struggle through the word-glut of curriculum guides. But what then? Have they got the picture? Admittedly, probably yes. What *is* the picture, though? It is, in most instances, a tortuously detailed, but incomplete mosaic which literally outdoes itself in the areas of literature, grammar, and vocabulary, and by comparison is abstruse about, and not infrequently treats the area of active communication (written and oral expression), with a few cavalier brushstrokes. It is in this area that curriculum guides become unrealistically presumptive, completely ignoring the vital matter of *how frequently composition is to be taught,* and often becoming manifestly vague about the kind of developmental sequence that is to be followed in its teaching. Therefore, they presume.

Curriculum guides presume that all English teachers know precisely what is expected of them in the teaching of composition. They presume that all English teachers will organize their teaching to make comprehensive composition programs possible. And they also presume that all English teachers will do so even though such programs entail large quantities of exacting and time-consuming work. The lattermost presumption, at the very least, is notoriously unwarranted when one considers the modern-day problem of heavy enrollments. Which brings us to . . .

Oversized Classes: The Crisis-Maker

"My classroom runneth over," laments today's teacher. "If I weren't making $8,000 a year, I'd be tempted to quit."

Have you thrown your hands up in despair at the throngs of youngsters that fill your classroom to overflowing each year? As the numbers increase or remain uncomfortably large, fall after fall, the temptation is almost overwhelming to forget about teaching and bone up on baby-sitting techniques, isn't it? Aside from the fact that overstuffed classrooms tend to depersonalize education, they pose still another very special problem for you, and it is a serious one, *primarily because its effects are felt largely in the area you as an English teacher should be most deeply concerned with—oral and written composition.* Obviously, the larger the class, the less frequent will be your students' opportunities for oral presentation. On the other hand, the problem that large classes pose relative to written composition need effect very little harm to your students, but certainly can to you in terms of work load—*unless you are able to settle on a regimen which allows you to spend most of your out-of-class time correcting student writing.* Easier said than done. Which brings us to . . .

Trivia: The Seducer

If all the impertinent tasks, academic and nonacademic, the average English teacher engages in were laid end to end, I couldn't think of a better fate for them, provided they were left there. Think of the reams and reams of grammar drillwork you've labored over down through the years, the masses of weekly, quarterly, and semester quizzes and exams you've passed judgment on, the thousands of grades you've averaged up. Consider the endless hours you've spent collecting fees and student-picture money; passing out and collecting various and sundry flyers for the PTA, the recreation and health departments, guidance, the principal's and vice-principal's offices, et cetera. It is a wonder you haven't had a breakdown by now.

As rational human beings, we should be constantly devising ways of ridding ourselves of such trivial tasks or at least reducing their numbers. But each succeeding year, alas, we seem to steep ourselves in them more and more. If by some diligent stroke we have managed to eliminate one or more of them, whether academic or nonacademic, others appear to take their place, occupying great chunks of our valuable time and energy, which might well be spent on more important tasks—education, for instance.

Examine, if you will, the correction of grammar drillwork. Besides being sleep-conducive, it is nothing more than a means of communicating largely irrelevant facts to your students, at the same time automatically dividing them into groups—those who in various degrees know subjects, complements, direct objects, verbs, verbals, clauses, and modifiers when they see them, and those who do not. Oddly enough, these groups reunite when it comes time for composition, for by some mysterious quirk, when writing and speaking, students all seem to know where these things belong.

Then there is that ubiquitous nuisance, the test. You must compose it, type up a master, run off sufficient copies, administer it, correct it, score it, and record it. The process, repeated over and over in the course of an academic year, can take on gargantuan proportions.

And what a morass of meaningless detail our grade-oriented minds have gotten us into! "Hominy A's j' git?" sounding through the corridors at report card time, has a terribly hollow ring. For what is the grade, after all, but another of our twentieth-century myths. It is arrived at unempirically and often arbitrarily. It creates fear, dissension, and snobbery, and it detracts from the real goals of education. But the more we talk of getting rid of it, the more things we find to grade. We are lately even grading homeroom. Who is to say that tomorrow it will not be lunch or rest room?

I suppose these things are halfway tolerable when one compares them with the many nonacademic administrative irritations which plague us: Two or three weeks of every semester collecting and recording monies for school fees; another two or three weeks of similar busywork with student pictures; repeated distributions of a dizzying assortment of flyers, copies of revised dress codes, tickets for school dances, et cetera. And of course there are the oft-repeated lectures about expected behavior in the lunch line and cafeteria, and in the library and corridors, and in the rest rooms and out on the playground. All during a period of the day which could be a time of uninterrupted study —for student and teacher alike.

Recognize the three heads? Of course you do. Anyone who has taught for any length of time is all too familiar with them and can probably describe them more aptly than I have. Paradoxically, putting a finger on the marplot they belong to is a much more elusive undertaking. Recognizing its potential as a negative force in education is even more difficult, *but our beast, Oblivia, nonetheless can, and I believe has, lulled a great many of us into a kind of infectious and sometimes blissful unawareness of why we are teaching language.*

And yet, isn't the reason all too apparent? Aren't we teaching language simply because it is a marvelously efficient and entertaining way to communicate? And aren't there two fundamental dimensions to communicating: listening and being listened to? Shouldn't they be considered equally important? Then why, in our classrooms, are so many of us emphasizing *passive* at the expense of *active* communicating? Which brings us right back to where we started: *It is because most English curriculum guides allow it; heavy enrollments seem to rationalize it; time-consuming trivia apparently necessitate it.*

An Analysis

There seems to be a tacit understanding between the curriculum guide and English teachers that as long as the goals for all the facets of a language course are enumerated, especially those for oral and written composition, however we reach them is unimportant—and if we never reach them at all, better luck next year. In effect, the guide says English teachers are to make the final judgment as to just how much active communicating their students get involved in while they are in their classrooms. Which is tantamount to saying (conditions being what they are), "Give them as much composition as you have time for, whenever you can sneak it in, and if you can give your assignments some kind of sequence, all the better."

Unfortunately, the guide, by implication, leaves very little time for composition. It designates a usually voluminous grammar text for use in language analysis, and though its exercises are long, numerous, and tedious and considered always entirely apart from composition, we tend to assign all of them or most of them to our students because the guide tells us to, or at least doesn't tell us not to. Granted, the grammar text is beginning to devote more of its pages to some kind of a composition program, but have you noticed how many of the exercises seem to be less challenging and imaginative with each new publication? The guide further jeopardizes the possibility of a comprehensive composition course when it goes on to delineate texts to be used and subject matter to be taught, with regard to literature. Its scope is often so unrealistic that, if followed, it would virtually preclude exploration of any other phase of language learning in the classroom. Vocabulary, with its ever-present, ponderous, time-consuming workbook, devours at least another full period of every week—pushing composition still further to the back of the shelf.

As if the temptations from the guide to neglect composition aren't great enough, along come jumbo-sized classes to furnish us with an even more "legitimate" reason for that neglect. How in heaven's name can we be expected to evaluate 150 or 200 pieces of student writing a week, or every two weeks, or every month, or even every quarter, when we have all this grammar drill and these mountains of quizzes and tests to correct, and so many grades to average? And where will we ever find the time for oral presentations with so many students? Since so few would be able to perform, what sense is there in doing it at all?

Now, I think it is at this point that so many of us are seduced. Because "all this grammar drill, and these mountains of quizzes and tests to correct, and so many grades to average" is essentially the language of trivia. And trivia can seduce, because so often it is clothed in the radiant garb of work. Ergo: if we must work so hard and accomplish so little, the gods must be against us.

How We Nurture Our Monster

Well, not really—just our three-headed hydra. And if we are aware of the fact, it is certainly not noticeable. We perpetuate the abstruseness of curriculum guides; we do little or nothing to soften the impact of large classes; we occupy hour upon hour of our valuable time with trifling matters as if our lives depended on it. No wonder we seem to be oblivious of our place in the scheme of things. Could it be possible that we are oblivious of the causes of our oblivion? I am virtually certain the opposite is true, yet I must confess my faith is shaken when I listen to some of the commentary which flies across the room at faculty meetings: "How come the science department gets to give its tests on Wednesday and the English department has to wait until Friday?" "Why do we have to make out the report cards in red ink?" "Students aren't getting to their first-hour classrooms early enough. Please advise." "Are black denims on boys alright?" "How long a detention for gum-chewing?" "Is it alright to use the green corridor pass if you can't find your yellow one?" "Don't you think we ought to change the name of the unsatisfactory report to something less negative?" "Where does guidance get off telling me how to discipline a student?" "When will our checks be in the office?" Sound familiar?

Can you remember a recent faculty meeting that turned out to be a forum for idea exchange among teachers, *relative to the education of youth and the solutions to academic problems?* I hope so. Have you ever talked among yourselves about the possibilities of a different approach to the writing of curriculum guides? How many times have you discussed practical ways of making large classes seem less large? When was the last time you collectively evaluated the merits of different kinds of tests or heard the suggestion that there were perhaps too many of them given? Is the possibility of eliminating grades or de-emphasizing them ever brought up? I should think this is what staff meetings are for. When else do we all get together? Are we or are we not in the business of education?

Judging from the plethora of committees we have brought into existence in the educative society, we would have to admit to the fact that something significant seems to be going on behind all those ivy-covered walls. If numbers mean anything, we should have eliminated practically all of our problems and perhaps even some of the federal government's by now.

Of course, like the number grade on a test, a committee lends an aura of importance to something which is often really not very important at all. Before you relegate me to the stake for that remark, think back to your last committee meeting. Was what went on there *really* significant enough to education to warrant regular meetings? Did you and the others engage in useful or even pertinent idea exchange and come up with substantive recommendations for the improvement of the educative society? Pay close attention to what goes on at the next committee meeting you attend, and as objectively as possible, weigh the important against the unimportant business that transpires there. If coffee is served, I should guess the affair will not be a total loss.

The gods are against us? How could they be when we are giving them so much to chuckle about? This is hardly a laughing matter, though. If we cannot even be lucid about the subject matter and skills we are to teach our students, there is no cause for laughter. If we have allowed ourselves to be bullied into submission, and even inaction, by large classes, there is nothing humorous in that. If we choose to be deluged by trifling tasks, then more's the pity. The gods may be chuckling; we have cause for sorrow.

And what about our students? Have they cause for sorrow? It is they most of all who should lament, but I suspect many of them are simply confused. And why not? Can we assume for a moment that those bright-eyed youngsters passing through our classrooms year after year don't suspect there is something amiss in our English programs? Don't you think they find it strange, for instance, that during one school year they may do considerable work in composition, and in another, practically none? Or that for weeks at a time they diagram scores of textbook sentences, but seldom or never compose a group of related ideas of their own? Or that they spend the better part of three days a week on vocabulary study, but never really get to use words in creative oral and written expression? I wonder if they know they are not being taught all of their language? Are they conscious of the random nature of their language learning?

Well, whether our students know it or not, our casual approach to the teaching of language is doing them irreparable harm. With respect to attitudes alone, I believe it has brought about alienation to the point where English is regarded as a necessary evil of formal education. It is tolerated. How many students do you suppose would pursue the subject in high school, for instance, if it were an elective? For that matter, in junior high? Have you ever stopped to ponder the hidden implications of that oft-heard remark, "I'm gonna be an engineer; why do I need English?" Is that really just "kid talk" or are students trying to tell us something? Might they in effect be saying, "My English courses aren't doing a very good job of teaching me how to use the language, so what relevance do they have to any other part of my education?"

We need only look on our college campuses to see the havoc a half-taught language is doing in terms of freshman dropouts. The correlation is alarming. Thousands of young college entrants every year just can't make the grade *simply because of their inability to compose a written language unit.* They are virtually incommunicado.

I believe, in large part, we English teachers have made them that way. That in itself is unfortunate to say the least. That so many of us are apparently oblivious of the fact is tragic. Tragic for our students, who have the right to expect of the profession a well-balanced professional program which stresses active communicating skills at least equally with passive communicating skills, *consistently throughout their formal education,* but who are instead learning their language piecemeal, subject all too often to the whims of English teachers and the vagaries of curriculum guides. Tragic for education, the goals of which are so obviously and irrevocably tied to the language arts. For without effective communication how can there possibly be effective education?

A Way Out

Well, how do we break out of this seemingly impossible and, most certainly, unedifying situation? How do we in effect at least emasculate our hydra? It *is* our creature, you know. In large part we created it—three heads and all. So, theoretically, what we have helped to create and admittedly are forced to co-exist with, we can nonetheless control. For with coexistence there is at least hope, hope that while coexisting we can, with appropriate strategy, render our hydra relatively harmless.

Transcending the Guide

About that curriculum guide. I don't suppose for a minute that English departments are going to consciously even consider taking steps to decrease the bulk or increase the clarity of this sacred cow of education. Curriculum committees too often are largely made up of overoccupied teachers who did everything they could to stay off the committee in the first place. Which in the second place, results all too frequently in their merely expanding on the previous guide, parroting much of its language. It would seem, then, that curriculum guides will change only when and if we can destroy all those presently in existence and start from scratch. And that, of course, isn't going to happen either—unless you want to get the ball rolling with some concrete proposals of your own at, say, your next faculty meeting. Pose the question of why there is nothing said specifically about frequency of composition assignments in the guide. Ask your colleagues for their ideas about the importance of oral and written communications in education generally, and language mastery, specifically. Could curriculum guides be made less cumbersome, less pedantic, more forthright? What would be wrong with an instruction outline guide such as the following?

COMPOSITION: Writing

SEQUENCE: 1. Three to twelve assignments at the level of single-paragraph development. 2. At least four multi-paragraph assignments. 3. Combination of all types of writing for the remainder of the year. 4. Explore poetry writing at conclusion of poetry survey in literature some time during the first semester.

SCOPE: 1. Paragraph development includes expository, descriptive, and persuasive writing. 2. Multi-paragraph assignments explore narrative writing, with emphasis on dialogue and descriptive detail. 3. Remaining assignments include options, but have enough specificity to balance single-paragraph and multi-paragraph assignments more or less equally. 4. Assign poetry at your discretion, always leaving students with an option to write prose if they so choose.

FREQUENCY: At least once a week for the entire year.

METHODS: 1. Assign compositions to be done over a two-day period, entirely in the classroom and preferably in pencil. 2. Collect incomplete compositions at end of first day and return to students the following day. 3. Begin giving individual help to students on first day and continue practice through the second day. 4. Collect finished compositions on second day. 5. Correct and return the following day.

And so on, for each phase of language curriculum—without all the prestigious language about goals. In this kind of direct language, nothing is so obvious as goals. If you are a member of a curriculum committee, all the better. The group is smaller and your proposals will have greater chance for a hearing. Quite probably, any such talk as this is going to be met with stares of incredulity, and perhaps even undisguised hostility, from some of your colleagues. Change seldom occurs in a cordial atmosphere, although ideally it should. If nothing comes of it, you at least have had the satisfaction of proposing something for the betterment of education. And don't drop the matter forever with a God-knows-I-tried attitude. Bring it up again and again. Sooner or later, you are going to precipitate some collective action by at least a part of the group.

Meanwhile, we and the curriculum guide must live together. It is probably not going to change substantially, and if it does, it will be a long process. But we can change. To begin with, we might re-examine some values by asking ourselves if the kind of English course we are offering is balanced. Is it as emphatic about the active dimension of communicating (writing and speaking) as it is about the passive dimension (reading, grammar, and word study) ? For most of us (and who needs a curriculum guide to tell us this?) , I think the answer to that question is going to be no. Inevitably, if our examination continues, there will follow several even more perplexing questions: What then of our role as teachers of language? If *we* cannot teach all of the language, who can? And what of our students? Do they count for anything? The answers to these questions are not found in curriculum guides either; they lie within us as teachers, and it is we who must answer them. In short, since we cannot ignore the curriculum guide or change its nature appreciably, we must transcend it.

And how do we transcend it? It's really rather simple: by counterpresumption, if I may use that term. Since the curriculum guide has presumed (I daresay with tongue in cheek) that we are going to teach all of the language, but has not clearly defined the way in which we are to do that—indeed, in many instances has made it virtually impossible for us to do so—then we must presume that its presumption is invalid. We must presume that the guide is not telling it how it is, and that under those circumstances we have a duty to act as our own guide. By doing so, honestly, we can effectively inactivate head number one of our hydra, which must ultimately lead to an attack on and the subsequent inactivation of the other two heads. For if we decide to teach *all* of the language in spite of the guide, we must inevitably find ways and means of softening the impact of large classes and eliminating much of the trivia in our teaching lives.

Alleviation of the Pain of Large Classes

"Alleviation" has to be the correct and qualifying term here, for the only way one can eliminate the agony of excessive enrollments is by reducing student numbers to a point where they no longer cause pain. And it is apparent that there is in the vast majority of our public school systems no substantial reduction of class sizes on the immediate horizon. Therefore, it seems obvious we are going to have to modify the symptoms until such time as major surgery can be performed.

The philosopher was right when he said "education is accompanied by pain." The word "pain," however, I don't think was meant to apply only to those being educated, and he didn't qualify it with "excruciating," which is the kind that often accompanies large classes, and applies, not to students necessarily, but almost exclusively to teachers. It is incumbent, then, it seems to me, for every teacher of whatever subject, to *lessen* the pain of class loads however he can, short of ignoring his duties, or resorting to drugs or suicide.

It is safe to assume, I suppose, that most of you are burdened with too-large numbers of students. The phenomenon has become a way of life in public school education. But have you met the problem head-on? The simplest and most effective way I have found, so far, to cope with it is the staggered-weekly-schedule system. It is so simple, as a matter of fact, that I blush to even talk about it, but not as much as I used to, however, since I recently discovered how few of my teaching acquaintances use it. The method adapts very well to the English teacher's regimen *and can make the possibility of frequent composition in his classes a reality.*

Let me be specific. What follows is an example of this kind of weekly program for five English classes. If you have never used this technique, I suggest you study it carefully. If you do use it, I would guess that it does for you what it does for me; that is, it allows for highly efficient use of time and maximum organization of each phase of your course:

Monday	Tuesday	Wednesday	Thursday	Friday
Second hour Grammar 15 minutes. Composition 40 minutes.	Composition 55 minutes.	Literature (anthology; novel).	Free reading ——————— Every other Thursday oral presentations and student-	Vocabulary study.

			oriented discussion.	
Third hour Vocabulary study.	Grammar 15 minutes. Composition 40 minutes.	Composition 55 minutes.	Literature (anthology; novel).	Free reading Every other Friday oral presentations and student-oriented discussion.
Fourth hour Free reading. ———— Every other Monday oral presentations and student-oriented discussion.	Vocabulary study.	Grammar 15 minutes. Composition 40 minutes.	Composition 55 minutes.	Literature (developmental reading).
Seventh hour Literature (anthology; novel).	Free reading. ———— Every other Tuesday oral presentations and student-oriented discussion.	Vocabulary study.	Grammar 15 minutes. Composition 40 minutes.	Composition 55 minutes.

Eighth hour				
Composition 55 minutes.	Literature (developmental reading).	Free reading. ——————— Every other Wednesday oral presentations and student-oriented discussion.	Vocabulary study.	Grammar 15 minutes. Composition 40 minutes.

Basically, the staggered schedule gives each of your five classes 95 minutes of written composition, 55 minutes of literature, 55 minutes of vocabulary study, and 15 minutes of grammar a week. Leisure reading and oral composition alternate 55 minutes each, every other week. I use the word "basically," because you are able, for various reasons, to inject elements of oral composition into your program on other days besides those designated. For example, the "free reading" day can be used for student-led discussion whenever it seems advantageous to your overall program. That one day, then, simply lends a degree of flexibility to your schedule that it might not otherwise have. In essence, this plan is an extension of what many elementary teachers use in the self-contained classroom, where I should think it would achieve the same fundamental effects.

As you can see, a schedule of this kind allows for a great deal of emphasis on oral and written composition—particularly the latter—because you, the teacher, never have more than one class's writing to evaluate on any given day. *It does require you, however, to settle into a day-by-day oriented regimen.* If, for example, you put off evaluating one class's writing for a day, you naturally find yourself the next day with writing to evaluate from two classes. In other words, with respect to writing (as with all other phases of your course), each class represents a different day of the week, and to stay ahead of the game, you must condition yourself to the rules. They are two in number: (1) finish all the papers you can during the school day; (2) take the rest home with you. Not exactly world-shaking as formulas go, but I assure you, an extremely workable one. With this kind of schedule, there are even days here and there when you can leave school knowing that you have only enough unfinished work on your desk to occupy you during your prep period the next day.

The system, as with any scheme, does have its drawbacks. In the area of literature, for example, a plan of this kind tends to create some discontinuity. Once you adopt it, though, I doubt that you will ever want to go back to the old way again. The old way might allow you to pursue a unit (if it is deemed important enough) every day of every week until you have finished with it—to the exclusion of everything else. In short, the old way makes possible near-absolute continuity with respect to any *one* facet of your language course, but over the long haul, creates discontinuity and sometimes outright chaos in the other areas of your language teaching. You achieve continuity in one area, but at the expense of the others. And with the old way, students and teachers not infrequently find themselves feasting distastefully on the same bulky portion of language over long periods of time, the experience possibly mesmerizing and self-defeating. But with the staggered schedule you have few opportunities for boredom; you are guaranteed variety in your day because every hour you are teaching a different facet of your language program. With this plan, there is also a stronger likelihood that in the course of a year you are going to get to teach *all* of the language. But most important of all, *the staggered system can effectively lessen the debilitating effect that large numbers of students have on you by dividing them into five distinct, more easily managed groups*—particularly from the standpoint of the written work they do for you in any given week. This gains added significance if you can manage to create a situation where composition is virtually the only thing you have to correct and evaluate outside of class. And it is possible!

Debureaucratizing Language Teaching

You and I would be less than candid if we did not admit to having consistently failed in our attempts to do away with the busywork of fee-collecting and other such administrative nuisances in our daily schedules. "You can't faze the malaise," as the saying goes. But we can do something about the administrative malaise we ourselves have created. There is the matter of exams and quizzes, for instance. If you find yourself all but perpetually occupied correcting test papers, your approach is hardly a rational one.

After all, what are exams and quizzes? Periodic "measurements" of student achievement, the results of which are expressed in terms of unempirical data called scores. Averaged in with all the other highly subjective data in your gradebook, they assume an unimportance second only to the dress and grooming code. *They are important mostly because we say they are important.*

What else do we know about tests? Well, they can be learning as well as measuring devices. But aren't perseverance and repeated exercise in a given skill, after all, the only realistic approaches to learning? And isn't the test supposedly just a confirmation of that learning? As such, is there any valid reason for scoring it, other than to have something to put in your gradebook?

Do away with tests? No, not necessarily, though I seriously doubt that education would collapse without them or the scores or letters that give them an importance they don't deserve. You could, however, eliminate much of your testing without in the least downgrading your language teaching. How could decreasing the number of tests you administer possibly hurt your students—unless your tests are without exception designed to teach as well as measure? And even if they were, would a few less, or even a lot less, really reduce the quality of learning that is going on in your classes? Ironically, the only answer I think you can give to that question is, "I don't know," which in my book is roughly equivalent to "No."

At any rate, that would be a good first step. Your second step could then be to devise tests which require an absolute minimum of time to administer and correct. Is there a good reason why any exam must take a student more than 15 minutes to finish or 30 seconds for you to correct? My students and I have settled on the multiple-choice form almost exclusively. Maximum correcting time for any of our tests is 10 minutes per class. Usually considerably less than that. Another of its advantages is that it is one kind of exam which can be made to teach as much as it tests—if any kind can.

Dumping Drillwork

Are you still correcting grammar drillwork? If you got a late start this afternoon, you probably are. (A little humor there.) A revolting task, isn't it? Then why do you do it? For years I asked myself that question periodically and never got a satisfactory answer. In short, correcting grammar drillwork had me talking to myself, and what is worse, expecting and getting answers—the wrong ones: "My students need to know their grammar, or else they won't be able to work their language. Therefore (yawn), I am correcting these papers." I was, of course, more or less parroting the words of all the teachers whose tutelage I had passed under. Well, I quit assigning and, hence, escaped the necessity of correcting grammar drillwork, having neither the inclination nor the money to consult an analyst. Why don't you too?

As a matter of fact, why require written grammar drill of your students at all, whatever kind it is? Copying sentences out of a book and parsing them, or diagraming them, or labeling them with pattern symbols, or bracketing the prepositional phrases is hardly going to make your students more effective communicators. Such activities merely serve as confirmation of usage: "So that's what they call this thing. Hey, look, mom, a prepositional phrase! Neat, huh?" If a student has diagramed or parsed a sentence or recognized its pattern, has he learned anything useful other than how to parse, or diagram, or recognize a sentence by pattern? And are such skills useful?

Now, if you make the decision to abandon written grammar drill, you can also very easily abandon the use of a text for grammar study and go to your students' writing for study material. Believe me, you will find the experiment highly gratifying and with each succeeding week, become more convinced of its complete practicability.

Eliminating Busywork

It has always seemed strange to me that grammar textbooks insist on drill exercises consisting of string after string of unrelated ideas. The important thing, apparently, is to come up with a sentence which posits the desired syntactical situation, as if this couldn't be done in the context of, for instance, a paragraph. Language has the precise function of effecting meaningful communications. Ironically, language textbooks (specifically grammar) are the only texts I know of that go about America mouthing such noncommunicative banalities as: "Donna fell down the stairs."; "Do you have any more stamps?"; "Ed's gyroscope is not working right."; "Please pass the oleomargarine." One might expect such utterances from a poorly programed robot, but a language text? It is easier and less stultifying by far to analyze language in the milieu of a student paragraph— and there is no drillwork for you to correct. More about this later.

Let it suffice to say here that if you really want to, you can eliminate a very large percentage of the time and busywork connected with grammar study and still confidently send your students on to the next grade with the fundamental knowledge of syntax their teacher will expect them to have. This, unfortunately, seems to be the only reason for teaching the stuff at all.

Downgrading the Grade

Is there a better place to start eliminating grades than in the English classroom, where student activities are so often (or should be) the kind that just will not adapt to a number or letter measurement? Admit it; the more creative writing you hand back to your students, the more senseless that letter grade (or grades) at the top seems, doesn't it? How can you measure creativity in mathematical terms or with letters that symbolize number values? Does a grade make any more sense relative to an oral presentation? If you devise a tool which points out the merits and weaknesses of a student's performance before his classmates, is there any need for a grade at all? Can't he draw his own conclusions from the evaluation if he insists there must be a grade?

I have a sneaking suspicion that our grading system would have died a natural death years ago had we not lost sight of education's goals. Stuffing students with knowledge is not one of those goals—unless the knowledge is used continuously in creative, communicative ways. Yet, stuffing students seems to be one of education's prime objectives. Now, you can readily find ways to measure stuffing, but it is not nearly so easy to place a number on creative communications. Hence, the more student-stuffing, per se, the more need for a grade, because there is something about a grade which lends relevance to the irrelevant.

Experience should have convinced us by now that in an English classroom the grade has little if any relevance. Then why not get rid of it wherever you can? Just a comment and a few revision symbols are all your students need to get on their compositions. A check sheet indicating strengths and weaknesses is all that is necessary for any oral presentation they make. Try it. It has only one disadvantage that I know of; your students will gripe about it for a time, but shortly they will adjust to the idea. The advantages, on the other hand, are almost too numerous to mention: the "stigma" of anything lower than a "B" is gone; students comparing papers can only judge by the merits of the compositions themselves; the ungraded paper on bulletin board display is there to be read, not to boast; the irritating task of trying to arrive at a fair judgment of a student's job of self-expression in alphabet symbolisms no longer plagues you, and such questions as, "Why did I get such a low grade?" are things of the past.

Unfortunately, your school still very likely issues subject-graded report cards and requires at least some scored examinations. You can't escape entirely from the nuisance of grading any more than you can expect substantially smaller classes. But where you *can* eliminate grading, I see no valid reason for not doing so. The rest you must live with—in as peaceful coexistence as possible.

You see, our hydra, though a formidable adversary, is nevertheless vulnerable. By "defanging" its three heads we can render it relatively impotent to do its malignant work—that of making mediocre English teachers of us. The beast only needs someone to challenge it. As teachers we are the only logical choice to do so, for we are the only ones who can possibly be intimately familiar with its tactics. The trouble is, we have been waiting all these years for someone else—the administration, the taxpayer, the government, *anybody*—to mount the attack, when all the time the challenge has been ours, and ours alone, to accept.

SUMMARY

1. As English teachers, you are confronted with a threefold problem: First, the curriculum guide, which presumes you are going to teach all of the language without furnishing you all of the specifics. Secondly, excessive numbers of students, which compounds the problem created by the guide. And thirdly, administrative and self-spawned trivia, which occupies so much of your time that it is virtually the straw that breaks the camel's back.

2. Perpetuation of curriculum guides in their present form; failure to take measures which will lessen the debilitating effects of unwieldy classes; and insistence upon continued trivial activities, such as excessive testing, assigning and correcting of meaningless grammar drillwork, and constant grading, manifest an apparent unawareness of the problem.

3. But there is a way out: Transcend, alleviate, de-bureaucratize. Three good action verbs, and they express in a nutshell the means by which you can emasculate that monster called Oblivia.

4. The first step of your attack must be a realistic interpretation of the curriculum guide and assumption of such tasks of language teaching as it has neglected or is vague about, particularly in the areas of oral and written expression.

5. To make possible the kind of total language program such an assumption necessitates, your next target should be large classes. One effective way to relieve their numbers burden is to stagger your weekly language schedule: Segment your course and assign each phase of it to a different day for each class.

6. Your third and final target, trivia, is considerably more vulnerable. Simply cut down the length and numbers of your tests; do away with written drillwork in grammar and minimize the time spent on grammar study generally; abolish grading wherever you can.

7. Before such an attack, if it is to be effective, there must be critical self-examination: Am I teaching all of the language or just nearly all of it? Do I regard large classes as something to be dealt with, or have I allowed myself to be intimidated into inaction by them? Is most of what I do in my classroom education, or am I preoccupied with the unimportant in my teaching?

2

Teaching Writing in a
Laboratory Atmosphere

In these early pages, you and I, I hope, have been communicating about our mutual problems, the urgency of their resolution, and what it can effect in terms of better education—specifically in the language arts. I daresay at this point we are clear as to what the problems are, or rather, what I contend they are. While I have also suggested remedies, their plausibility can become really clear only in terms of the kind of language program they make possible. In the ensuing pages, we are going to take a detailed look into one such program.

Our first look will be at the kind of oral and written composition programs our proposed remedies can make possible. Further on, we will view the study of grammar for exactly what in large part it is—trivia, and how our proposed remedies can make it relatively painless, but certainly no more ineffective than it has ever been. Our view of vocabulary study will suggest alternatives, but the gist of the program described will reflect the elimination of at least some of the unimportant activities that have been part and parcel of it in the past. And the literature program we are going to look at clearly mirrors—at least in its broad scope and pragmatic approach—the effects of our proposed remedies.

Taken as a whole, the program we are about to explore would be impossible without the remedial action suggested in Chapter 1. It is a program which deals with language learning realistically, I believe. And it is a fluid program, which changes each year —often drastically—and it will continue to change. I think change is a prerequisite for any good teaching program, because I can think of nothing worse for education than a teacher stalled on dead center.

I should like to suggest that the program's prime strength is that it is student oriented; I believe that in a student-oriented program you are only the catalyst, and a relatively silent one at that. Not that you are unimportant. You *are* important, of course, and your importance lies to a great extent in knowing *when to stop telling your students how to do and when to begin letting them do.* And student-doing is really what most of the rest of this book is about.

Composition: The Orphan of Language Teaching

There is much talk in education these days about curriculum enrichment, most often referred to in terms of larger teaching staffs and/or added materials, such as: textbooks, educational television, language labs, tape recorders, electronic duplicators, overhead projectors, record-players, bigger and better flickers, et cetera. Reduced to these terms, curriculum enrichment is in essence a budgetary matter; because of the economic bind in which most educational institutions find themselves, "enrichment" remains (a good percentage of the time) just talk. In large part, enrichment of any phase of curriculum must result from "teacher power": *It is what you do with what you have that can enrich any facet of your teaching.* All these other things are more or less incidental.

Now I can think of no surer way to enrichment than the

development of a comprehensive writing program in your English classroom. And all that is needed is students, pencils, paper, an organized writing unit, and you.

From the students' standpoint, frequent written self-expression simply means fulfillment of an innate human desire to create. That should be reason enough for such a program. But writing is also an exercise in thinking and organizing. And by no means least important, it is another way your students can get to know themselves a little better.

From your standpoint, this kind of enrichment is just as significant: You have been given the most important task in America today, that of making the nation's youth better communicators. In order to do that, you have to develop in your students both dimensions of the art of communicating—the active dimension and the passive dimension. Full development of each, it seems to me, is about all the enrichment a language program needs. But this enrichment is significant for you in still another way. Through maximum development of active communicating in your students, you, in effect, have a built-in liaison between them and you, which, it would seem, is one excellent way to slow down the present rate of depersonalization in today's education. For through active communicating, you can become acquainted with each of your students in a way you couldn't otherwise possibly know them.

For these reasons, it seems to me this area of English curriculum is the most vital. And yet, paradoxically, it is also, I believe, the most grossly neglected, which fact in itself constitutes, to say the least, a first-rate problem. As has been pointed out, the English curriculum guide not infrequently helps create the problem by seldom talking turkey about written communications in the English classroom, the consequence being *that it is this vital activity that students engage in the least while they are learning their language.*

At the risk of heresy, I must say I think all curriculum guides should be followed with tongue in cheek, unless, of course, by some inexplicable turn of events, they should suddenly come to grips with reality. I would, for instance, be thoroughly enchanted with a school system which formulated a structured, sequential writing program for grades 1 through 12, expressed in language which suggests not what might be taught, but what had very well better be taught. Students can hardly learn how to express themselves capably if they are not given the opportunity to do so; teachers are not going to teach communications skills the way they should be taught unless they are given explicit instructions on how and how often they are to be taught. In short, enriched curriculum should produce a language program in which written communications skills are taught frequently —I should think no less than once a week; taught consistently —at every grade level; taught sequentially—gradually increasing in sophistication; and taught relentlessly—every week of every school year, *with the specifics of the program set down in the guide in clear, unmistakable language.*

The classic objection to this kind of program is the "class-loads-don't-allow-it" lament, and it is probably the objection heard most often. Another is the "I-don't-know-how-to-teach-writing" syndrome. Still another is the "frequent-writing-doesn't-necessarily-produce-good-communicators" philosophy. To the lattermost claim I think the obvious answer is, "How do we know?" I mean, for sure? How consistently and frequently did you and I engage in language manipulation as we came up through the grades? Have any of us really been on the receiving end of a concentrated, structured, sequential writing program during our formal education—even for a year, let alone 12? Ask your students this fall—any fall—about their most recent exposure to it in an English classroom. The most recent survey I took revealed that 60 per cent of my students had done work in written composition less frequently than once a month during the previous year, and 75 per cent of them had done virtually nothing in the way of oral presentation.

Admittedly, there has been considerable research done in this area, some of which seems to indicate that frequent writing doesn't improve a student's ability to communicate, some of which seems to indicate that it does. *If education really wants to find out, the best way I can think of is to teach, really teach, writing in its schools.*

The other two objections don't leak quite so much water, but they can hardly be called valid. The class-loads lament, I blush to admit, lethargized me early in my career, but I soon regained consciousness and reasoned that relatively large classes seem to be with us on a more or less permanent basis. So to beg off teaching communications skills because of too many students seemed rather like holding out for another education system. The alternative was surrender to reality. In all honesty I had to choose the latter course, the consequences of which were hardly catastrophic, resulting as they did in my students and I gradually settling on a regimen which allows us maximum concentration on what to me seems the center of gravity of any language course —the development of at least adequate skill in active communicating. The formula is reasonably simple: (1) we have abandoned much of the trivia—that is, the irrelevant—which blights so much of today's teaching; (2) we have adopted the staggered-schedule system (See Chapter 1), which simply means I have only one class's writing a day to pass judgment on. For example, a first-hour class writes on Monday and Tuesday, a second-hour class on Tuesday and Wednesday, et cetera, the entire assignment done in the classroom in pencil from the rough-through-subsequent drafts, right up to the final draft and proofreading. Why not a take-home? You may do it that way, if you wish, but I think it turns out in too many instances that spontaneity suffers, and you cannot always tell when you are communicating with the student, and when with the parent. At any rate, with the classroom writing plan you are always at your students' disposal *while they are writing,* and this is precisely when the teaching of syntax (in anything but syntactical language, by the way) becomes most pertinent—when the student is composing a meaningful unit of language.

But by far the most compelling reason for classroom-contained composition lies in the nature of the task itself. To begin with, writing is an extremely exacting business. It calls for your presence, giving all the help you possibly can to individual students and as many as possible over the two-day period. It is hardly realistic to assume your young writers are going to scrutinize carefully and therefore learn writing skills from the annotations you scribble on their returned papers. You have got to catch them in the act, so to speak. In order to do that, you have got to get *into* the act. Take-home assignments automatically eliminate your *personal* participation.

But what about the teacher who says he can't teach writing? I simply don't believe him. If I did, my advice to him would be to switch to driver-ed, and fast. Granted, we have all come up through an education system which seems to place little stress on creativity and practically none at all on communications skills, but it is the only education system we have, and who is going to teach these things if not us? The mandate is ours. Was there ever any doubt? If nothing else, we and our students can learn together, which after all is not a bad concept as concepts go.

Techniques

How does one teach writing, then? I can answer only on the basis of my own experience. The question seems terribly difficult to answer satisfactorily when you are talking about 150 or 160 students. However, it becomes far less formidable when you attempt to answer it in terms of a program with a realistic starting point, which is implemented on a given day of each week for each of your classes in an orderly sequence, allowing students to do more, and different, and increasingly complex things with their language—entirely in the classroom environment.

I assume (I believe, correctly) that the preponderance of my students each fall are ready in varying degrees to joust with single-paragraph development. I imagine yours are too. In fact, it would seem unwise to venture beyond one paragraph in most junior high school classes until about the middle of the second quarter, beginning with three or four assignments of description in as many weeks, stressing all the way the importance of unity (each sentence related in some way to the central theme) , continuity (logical sequence of ideas), use of the best possible diction (gut-words), and attractive style (student "trademark" arousing reader interest). In subsequent weeks, you can move on to exposition and persuasion—also in the context of the single-paragraph assignment. The number of weeks you spend on single-paragraph development, however, is entirely up to you. I should think that at the upper levels of high school, you could get by with less exposure to it, but I believe some is called for at every level of education—if only as a kind of warm-up exercise preliminary to more sophisticated writing activities.

By way of more specific information, here are the first 12 weeks of a year-long writing unit, the subject matter of which is suitable for junior high school. The format, however, is applicable to senior high school as well, with some modifications which will be described further along in the chapter:

A—Description
1. A paragraph describing a valued inanimate possession. Use as much detail as possible. If you have the object with you, all the better. If not, try to remember as much about its physical properties as possible.
2. A paragraph describing your favorite animal. This could be your dog, cat, goldfish, or merely some species of animal that you are particularly attracted to. Include character as well as physical traits.
3. A paragraph: You are your pet and you are writing about your master (you). Emphasize descriptive detail.
4. A paragraph describing yesterday's cafeteria lunch (including your reaction to it), or your own if you ate a cold lunch.

B—Exposition
1. In a paragraph, explain a skill you have, how you acquired it, and how it is performed. Combination can be important in carrying out this assignment.
2. In one paragraph, tell your reader what, as you see it, the so-called generation gap is.
3. Explain, on your own terms, the phenomenon of the sun rising in the east and setting in the west. (One paragraph.)

      4. An expository paragraph based on a literature reading assignment given the day before.

C—Persuasion

      1. In one paragraph, present your case for something you believe in strongly. You are trying to persuade your reader that your viewpoint is the correct viewpoint.

      2. In one paragraph, attempt to persuade your reader that dress and grooming are/are not matters for each individual to decide for himself.

      3. In one paragraph, attempt to persuade your reader that manned explorations of the moon are/are not worthwhile.

      4. A paragraph in which you try to persuade your reader that _____ in the story _____ acted as he did from selfish/unselfish motives. (In conjunction with literature assignment given the day before.)

With your first assignment, you talk about descriptive writing, generally, and move to specifics about the task at hand—description of a valued possession. Remind your students that in writing anything original, they are really producing order out of chaos; then have them first jot down all the describable features of their possession. The results might turn out to be something like the following:

My Bike

White and gold; badly bent and scratched fenders; left brace from front axle to front fender broken; one broken seat spring, left side; taped grips on handlebars; originally ten-speed sprocket, now only three; chrome rims dirty; lightweight, treadless tires; loose cyclometer on front wheel; light with no batteries; loose sprocket guard.

Your students now have the chaotic beginnings of their first paragraph assignment. From here you instruct them to organize their description, beginning (for simplicity's sake) with the thesis or topic sentence and following it with sentences, incorporating from their jottings the different features of the object being described. Illustrate on the chalkboard a variety of possible approaches to the opening sentence of this kind of paragraph: "My bike is in pretty bad shape, but it gets me where I want to go."; "I'll bet you never owned a bike as beat up as mine."; "About five years ago, Santa left a brand new shiny bicycle under our Christmas tree." It is extremely helpful to compose a short paragraph on the board at this juncture, perhaps describing something you own.

These first weeks, as you can see, deal with subject matter and idea development at a level that is almost painfully elementary. And for several of those weeks, you will have to repeat in large measure the instructional techniques you used for the very first assignment. The purpose behind all this is to get your students away from the notion that they can sit down and compose a unit of language on the first try. As you know, virtually all adolescents labor under this delusion. If in the first half dozen or so assignments you can get them into the habit of jotting down ideas at random relative to the writing task at hand, with a view to gradually organizing them into a coherent composition through subsequent drafts, it becomes a foregone conclusion before long that this is an effective way to write good, clear prose. And early in the program, there is no law that says you, yourself, can't do a bit of the jotting for individuals who are obviously at sea. You will be more than repaid for your efforts, as you discover they have helped not a few of your students get off on the right foot.

In any event, there is no other realistic approach that I know of if you hope to reach the great majority of your students. The repetition pays off and it becomes apparent when you reach more sophisticated levels of writing. The situation could be compared with that which you find in the early stages of a boxing match; both fighters are engaged in only the most elementary moves while studying the other's style and tactics. They "feel" each other out for a few rounds. This is what your students should be doing with their writing in these initial weeks.

Assuming for the moment your system has adopted a structured writing program for every year at the secondary level, you would gradually diminish the time spent on single-paragraph development at each grade level. For the tenth-grade level, six weeks' exposure might be appropriate; at the eleventh-grade level, perhaps three weeks. At the twelfth-grade level, depending on the caliber of your students, you might be able to begin immediately with various kinds of multi-paragraph assignments, or you might feel it necessary to start your writing program with perhaps two or three single-paragraph assignments.

Your writing unit, to be effective, I think, must change at least every other year, if not annually. The format can remain relatively static, but as new ideas for subject matter occur during the year, it is a good idea to jot them down and incorporate them into your program for the following year. Of course, you need not wait until the following year if you happen onto an exceptionally attractive addition and want to use it at the earliest possible date. A technique like this followed faithfully is practically a guarantee that your writing course will remain fresh and become increasingly conducive to student creativity.

The phrase "on your own terms," relative to assignment B-3 of the previously mentioned writing unit, is an example of this kind of thing. Adding that phrase to the assignment instructions, in effect adds options which allow students to explain in whatever entertaining way they choose—whether it be in scientific terms or otherwise—the phenomenon of sunrise and sunset. The options result in an astounding variety of approaches to the subject. An added bonus is that it gives students who really don't know exactly why the sun rises in the east and sets in the west a face-saving out.

Teaching Syntax Through Writing

It is in these early weeks of your writing program that you pay particularly close attention to problems of syntax in student writing. By giving them attention here, you pave the way for fewer problems later on when your students are performing more complex writing tasks. And this is that time we spoke of earlier when grammar instruction has real pertinence: A prepositional phrase, for instance, suddenly becomes significant when you point out to a student who is writing that he has one badly positioned, or an appositive, when you explain it is a transform and why it has to be set off by commas. How can the precise use for a pronoun be better explained than in a student's writing, where there is no identifiable antecedent for it? Could hours of instruction about dependent clauses be as effective as your reading a dependent clause fragment to the student who has just written one, and having him detect the absence of terminal juncture in your voice pitch? What amount of compound sentence identification could surpass a suggestion to the writing student that he combine two closely related sentences with a conjunction? Can the reason for transposition of sentences be shown more conclusively than when you demonstrate to a student how the use of one in his paragraph will help break up sentence sameness? Wouldn't you say the proper punctuation of a possessive noun has real significance in the context of a paragraph which also has "s" ending plurals in it? Have a student read a run-on sentence to you, and he will almost invariably orally punctuate it; ask him why he stopped and lowered his voice at a given point, and more often than not he will get the drift. Doesn't the search for strong verbs or more precise nouns or definitive modifiers teach the concept of word function far better than talking about them in terms of parts of speech? How important, for example, is the word "gerund" to the writing student who places it in a nominal position and prefers to call it a noun, or even a verb?

If your students do all their writing in the classroom, under your surveillance, you have as many opportunities as you could ever want, to teach them syntax—and most frequently on a one-to-one basis. But you don't even have to mention that unpleasant word, grammar. You can travel from desk to desk and suggest improvements in word and sentence relationships, and your students will be cognizant only of the fact that you are trying to help them with their writing. They will never suspect you are teaching them grammar—which would seem to be some kind of a victory for our side.

Creativity Within the Paragraph

The question invariably arises of how creative junior and senior high school students can be in one paragraph. Aside from the fact that all original writing is creative (in the philosophical sense) but not necessarily imaginative, the question, I think, is moot. The teacher's goal need hardly be the production or discovery of adolescent Twains, or budding young Thoreaus, but should one or the other come along, he would find the paragraph as good a vehicle as any for his talents. For example:

> Our society's aversion to work is terribly noticeable. Say work to any typical 14-year-old and you'll see an automatic recoil of horror, followed by an outbreak of nervous hives. We're allergic to work! It's a nasty word to us. We stifle a chuckle at the family reunion when the old-timer tells about how he would "chop four cords of wood and then do some hard chores—before breakfast." Horrors! Send a 1970 kid to carry out the garbage and you'll get a look of sheer martyrdom, heartbreaking enough to melt a Nazi SS man. What ever happened to work? Where along the path to glory did we discard it? Didn't it suit us? Along the way we've also lost peace and serenity. Is it merely a coincidence that work is passé and now peace is gone? Haven't we lost them both? [1]

The young essayist who wrote that happens to represent the distaff side. She is a dynamic, vibrant youngster who I can't possibly imagine being in a class where she is not asked to write frequently. She came into my class with an affinity for writing, and she left, I hope, with at least the same kind of ability. She didn't need me—*except to make her exercise that gift of hers*—but I needed her, because it is this kind of student that makes teaching writing skills to adolescents just that much more rewarding.

Admittedly, this breed of student is the exception, but then in one way or another isn't every student? Look at this from one of my morning classes of several years back:

> What do people have against long hair on boys? Long hair doesn't mean we're no good. Not everybody with long hair goes out and causes trouble. It gives us a sense of security if our hair hangs down on our foreheads and is thick at the sides. Besides, why do you teachers care, anyhow? It's *our* hair. You've got your own hair to work with—most of you, anyway. Would you come to school in a colored sport shirt? You would probably feel insecure

---

[1] Sandra Buchberger is the authoress.

and unnatural without a white shirt and coat. Long hair is the style, and you stand out if you haven't got it. Our generation has got something good going, and I hope it lasts.[2]

From the male of the species, a young fellow with a thoroughly "normal" coiffure, as I recall, whose talent for writing over the year was generally unprovocative, though adequate, but who when asked to make social comment, was in his element.

Another member of the fair sex wrote this poignant piece of persuasion. On the day in question, I had given the class the rather elusive title, "We've Got a Complex," and told them simply to create a paragraph to go with it:

It seems to me that many people in our country today have a complex that makes them think violence is the only way to solve a problem. Too many people think that dropping more bombs on Viet Nam is going to end the war. Riots and lawless demonstrations seem to be a popular way of making a point. Political assassination has become a way of getting rid of people we don't agree with. Basically, America is a wonderful and compassionate country. But this atmosphere of violence is dividing us, and making us hate one another. What was ever accomplished by violence? Robert Kennedy said, "Violence breeds violence; repression breeds repression." I love my country and I cry inside every time we drop more bombs, every time a riot breaks out, and every time a man is shot, because I know that my country is hurt. We've got to tear down this atmosphere of violence. What the world needs now is love.[3]

One can overlook the mixed metaphor at the end in view of the effective style and tone of the paragraph as a whole. This young writer had a crusading spirit—virtually every assignment I gave, she somehow managed to turn into a plea for sanity in the world.

How's this for some refreshing autobiography:

Worst Amateur Barber

I can remember way back when my father used to cut my hair. I wouldn't want to get a haircut at all. And it's the truth. But it

---

[2] Richard Johnson is the author.
[3] The authoress is Lisa Martin.

wasn't because I liked long hair. Matter of fact, nine years ago I wasn't sure what hair was. The reason I disliked the idea of my father cutting my hair was tied to what he did to my oldest brother. Why, my dad took a chunk out of my brother's ear big as my fingernail. Actually it was only a scrape, but when you're always looking up at everyone it doesn't look like just a scrape. Did dad have trouble getting me into that chair! But he finally managed. I was really suffering and I let him know it. So we guys decided then that we'd take no more chances. "Let us go to the barber shop!" we cried. Dad was happy to get rid of us, but he knew then that he was the worst barber of all time.[4]

The young author of that paragraph was not exactly a technician with syntax, and he was a little too vague and digressive at times, but entertaining, nonetheless. Although I never assign autobiography, per se, he seemed to prefer it, pursuing it every chance he got. I suppose because he was at his best then.

The thing is, given enough latitude over a long enough period of time, at frequent enough intervals, virtually every one of your students will find his niche. This should be one of our strongest arguments for a comprehensive writing program. We are constantly in search of something—anything—an individual can do well, and with a variegated writing program, you are all but bound to hit on some phase of it that one student or another finds himself particularly suited to. It might be the subject matter or the kind of writing that the assignment calls for, but he knows when you get there that this is his "bag."

Sequential Advancement

Rightly or wrongly, I think narrative writing is most effective beyond the one-paragraph stint, and so anywhere from the ninth to the twelfth week of your junior high school program you begin your multi-paragraph compositions (again, three or four consecutive assignments), emphasizing dialogue and descriptive detail. As pointed out earlier, the sequential advance from single-paragraph writing would come progressively sooner with each succeeding grade.

---

[4] Jim Neuwirth is the author.

The transition from single-paragraph to multi-paragraph assignments is not an easy one when a student is asked also to include dialogue. But I believe the leap is justified for several reasons. Experience will show you that advancing from the single-paragraph to the multi-paragraph composition is not highly progressive—especially when you are pressed for time anyway—unless you inject the dialogue element into it. Students generally are enthusiastic about getting into dialogue writing, for it allows them still more opportunities for creativity. Besides, most students apparently are ready for the leap; in any event, difficult though it is—particularly at the junior high school level—they adjust to it readily enough. I hasten to add that later on in their program the writing of multi-paragraph compositions without dialogue is called for by implication, where an assignment's flexibility leaves students with options.

Dialogue: Punctuation and Tone

This is an ideal time for some added and more concentrated instruction in the rules of punctuation, especially dialogue punctuation. Review of the uses of the comma is always in order; all students, as you know, have trouble with it. Then demonstrate on your chalkboard the correct use of quotation marks, the separation by the *comma value* of the *conventional* attributive from the quote, the necessity for indenting with each change of speaker where the dialogue is copious, the use of the *period value* in separating the *inferred* attributive from the quotation, and the use of single quotation marks around a quotation within a quotation. The most effective technique in teaching dialogue punctuation, it seems to me, is to compose a brief exchange on the board involving (for simplicity's sake) just two people. With a little prior organization on your part, you can have prepared a short dialogue which includes virtually every possible punctuation eventuality.

But it is really not the punctuation of dialogue that is so troublesome. Rather, it is creating a credible tone in the dialogue itself. This calls for skillful use of the attributive and its elimination when it is not really called for. It requires also an explanation of the differences between the conventional attributive and what might be called the inferred attributive which often contains considerably more descriptive detail. Specifically, the conventional attributive is almost always separated from the quote by the *comma value* (the comma value frequently being assumed by the question mark or exclamation mark), whatever their respective positions in the sentence:

"We are all in this thing together," *announced Eloise.*

"What right have you to speak for me, Ellie?" *asked Dexter, squinting warily from his position on the floor.*

The inferred attributive (and this is not so troublesome for students as it might seem) generally requires the *period value* to separate it from the quotation and is a natural vehicle for the insertion of descriptive detail within a narrative:

"From the start, Dexter, you, and all of you, knew what you were getting into." *Eloise's face was flushed and her fingers played nervously with the barrel of her pistol.*

Or, combining both kinds of attributive:

Dexter got to his feet, moved quickly to where Eloise was standing, and looked out over the group of campus dissidents sprawled in various positions in the corridor. "Are we going to let the dean's daughter tell us what to do?" *he asked.*

It is important, I think, to use that term *comma value* in reference to the instances of the question mark, the exclamation mark, as well as the comma itself, separating the conventional attributive from the quotation. It's important, because more than a few of your students are just going to insist on using a period in this kind of situation, and sometimes even double punctuation. If, however, you stress the comma value idea, I believe you will save yourself and your students much time and trouble during this phase of your writing program.

With subsequent narrative-with-dialogue assignments, these things have to be re-emphasized. Overuse of the conventional attributive is by far the most prevalent weakness of student writing in this facet of composition, so you would do well to give repeated brief instruction regarding the various dialogue situations which allow for elimination of the attributive altogether. One such situation is the two-person dialogue when initial speaker identity is required, but none thereafter, or at the most, re-establishment of it if the dialogue becomes lengthy. The noun of address is a useful substitute for the attributive and, of course, what a character is saying often identifies him:

> Eloise turned to Dexter and angrily cried, "You're a fink!"
>
> "Me, a fink! Look who's calling who a fink!"
>
> "Yes, a fink. You'd turn in your own mother to save your skin."
>
> "Are you suggesting I'm a coward?"
>
> "You said it, not me."
>
> "Look, Ellie, if you weren't wearing glasses I'd show you who's a coward."

And then there is the matter of broken quotations. This, too, is a troublesome area for youngsters. Again, the comma value and period value concepts are important here. The latter is always used following the attribual break in a multiple-sentence situation:

> "Like why don't you sit down, Dexter," snapped Eloise. "You're blocking the view."

The comma value always follows the attribual break in a one-sentence situation:

> "Okay," grumbled Dexter, "but don't expect me to testify for you at the Senate hearings."

For demonstration purposes, your chalkboard is the most effective instrument for communicating to your students the precise differences between the kinds of attributives, when it is possible to get along without any attributive at all, and how to properly punctuate broken quotations. No text that I know of even comes close to exploring all of the possibilities. Nonetheless, students need to know all of these things if they are going to write attractive narrative. *And they will understand them if you assume they can.* The assumption must be accompanied, however, by clear explanations, repeated in the course of their dialogue writing. With some of your groups, understanding is naturally going to come more quickly than with others, and some of your classes, of course, will not be capable of understanding more than the conventional attributive, if indeed you are able to venture into dialogue writing with them at all.

In this phase of the course, you will encounter additional difficulties in persuading your students of the necessity of indenting for every change of speaker. When there are only snatches of dialogue, it is generally not necessary to indent each new quotation, but when dialogue is more or less continuous, indentation for each change of speaker is imperative. By the end of their second dialogue assignment, most of your students will realize this and understand why it is so important. But you will still have some who continue writing their dialogue without the use of indentation. When you come alongside them at work, you are hard-pressed to understand why they cannot see just by looking at that mess of sparrows' feet jammed together chaotically on their papers, that all is not right. Don't sigh, though; they will do the sighing when you show them how it should have been done.

How do you communicate to any student the "casual" concept with regard to the dialogue itself? No amount of instruction about effective use of attributives is going to result in that credible tone we talked about earlier, if the utterances of the speakers themselves are written in stilted language. Some (happily, not many) students apparently have not gotten over their exposure to the reading material of the primary grades, where, as you well know, the storybook characters talk like no one we have ever known or are likely to know. And so, even from high school students you get the " 'Let us go fly a kite!' cried Jimmy" kind of thing occasionally. The few who resort to such jejune language you might attempt to instruct, using the let-your-hair-down psychology: "You don't talk that way and neither do your friends." Encouraging them to use more contractions and terms such as "gonna," "lotsa," and other everyday colloquialisms and slang expressions in their dialogue is helpful too, but it is extremely difficult to completely obliterate the indelible marks left by the primers.

Creativity Within Multi-Paragraph Writing

Given enough practice and help along the way, your students will come up with some very creditable productions in this challenging area of creative writing. The following is the result of an assignment which called for a dialogue involving three people or more. It is one of many collected which evidence the adolescent writer's ability—with enough practice and help from you—to understand the concept of casual tone and realize the variety of alternatives one has in choosing attributives:

The New Look

The professor smiled at Miss Wooster. "It'll be just a minute now. Mademoiselle Vigny is always late for appointments, except fashion shows, that is."

Mlle. Vigny entered the restaurant soon after. She hurried toward the table with outstretched arms. "My dears," she sparkled, "how wonderful of you! It's been so long since I saw Professor March. Oh, Professor, you must introduce me to your friend."

Professor March said courteously, "Miss Wooster, meet Mademoiselle Vigny." There followed a polite exchange of amenities and Mlle. Vigny sat down.

"Darling, your hat is delightful. But your dress! A woman like you should never wear such a thing. You should wear—an oriental look, perhaps? Yes, that would be better."

Miss Wooster, who had been wearing that "thing" for two years, simply smiled and spoke. "Would you tell us about the government you've helped to start?"

"But of course. Let's see, it started about one year ago. It was the year darling Oleg introduced the ankle trumpet flare. I'm sure you've seen it. In any case, everything started in March. That awful M. de Gaulle made some simply nasty remarks. He looked at Christian Dior's new gownlet fashion—enchanting, wasn't it— and said that it made women look absolutely unfeminine. He said Christian's models must be sculpted ice. He dared them to straighten up. He claimed they leaned backward so much they must use artificial backbones. Naturally we couldn't let such things go on. So, we simply removed him from office. We dropped ads in papers which printed news about him. We kept the heads of his cabinet busy at parties. We never spoke of him. Soon it spread to the middle classes. In six months, he was a forgotten man. After his resignation, we moved Andre Malraux into his spot. You see, it was simple."

"Yes, it was," commented Miss Wooster, looking quite amazed.

"And, of course, we soon returned to normalcy. That reminds me, how are the peach-blossom styles coming along out here?"

"Just fine, I suppose," replied Miss Wooster.

Two hours later, after a three-course luncheon and several fashion reviews, Mademoiselle Vigny departed.

"That's not the worst of it, either," said Professor March glumly. "Think of all the influential women wearing French styles. If it worked there, it will work anywhere."

Miss Wooster stared at him in rising horror as she remembered that a few days ago the President of the United States had referred to imported French fashions as "lifeless" and "unfeminine." [5]

Notice the excellent descriptive attributives and the natural flavor of the conversation, the correct use and punctuation of both kinds of broken quotation. Incidentally, you'll meet the young lady who wrote this again in a later chapter.

Expanding Your Base—An Eclectic Approach

With the narrative, you have completed what constitutes a base from which all further student writing stems—that is, in the area of prose. What follow then are variations of what has gone before; for example: "Develop a single paragraph with your central theme the human activity of eating."; "Compose a narrative with dialogue, created around the concept of faith."; "Write a multi-paragraph essay in which you attempt to persuade your reader that 18-year-olds should/should not have the

---

[5] Pamela Peterson is the authoress.

vote."; "You have full latitude this week. Create something to go with the title, 'Time Is Only Place.' "; et cetera. To illustrate this more clearly, here is the next 20-week segment following the single-paragraph phase of your program. It can be equally effective at both levels of secondary education:

D—Narration
  1. Write a dialogue involving two people. Include descriptive detail.
  2. Write a dialogue involving three or more people. Include descriptive detail.
  3. Write a narrative (dialogue included) titled "Friends."
  4. Take the two principal characters in the story, _____ _____, and make them the only characters in a story of your own. Include dialogue (in conjunction with literature assignment given the previous day).

E—Human Activities: Essay, narrative, with or without dialogue, single or multi-paragraph. Assignments varied throughout the weeks:
  1. Eating 2. Love 3. Fighting 4. Sleep 5. Play 6. Work 7. Communicating 8. Fear (a human activity also, unfortunately) 9. Dying.

F—Concepts: Essay, narrative, with or without dialogue, single or multi-paragraph. Assignments varied throughout the weeks:
  1. The universe 2. God 3. Faith 4. Immortality 5. The devil 6. Democracy 7. Integration.

The "D" section of this unit, after one year's trial, required change. An earlier version left out "Include descriptive detail" in assignments 1 and 2 and "dialogue included" in assignment 3. Before the year was out, I realized it would be necessary to include this additional instruction specifically, simply because too many of my students concentrated on the dialogue part to the exclusion of descriptive detail in the former and vice versa in the latter. In short, you have got to remind your young writers when they are engaged in narrative composition, that description is a vital ingredient, even if what they are writing is predominantly dialogue, and that the two in fact complement each other in any good story.

I heartily recommend sections "E" and "F" for your writing program. I still use them. As you can imagine, they result in some extremely entertaining creations, and I think it is apparent why. As pointed out earlier, their subject matter content allows for the broadest interpretation by your students and gives them maximum opportunity for imaginativeness.

Teaching Poetry

And what about poetry? We hardly mention it until we come to the poetry survey (early in the year) in the literature phase of our course—although when we get there, specific poetry assignments are given. Then those who wish to try their hand at it may do so. To those students (and they are numerous) who just can't seem to swing poetically, it would seem wise to give the option of prose.

Beginning with the tenth grade, I believe students should be taught some of the technical language of poetry. (See Chapter 6.) And this can be presented either in the literature or the composition phase of your program. I prefer the former procedure. If early in the year you spend a few weeks on a poetry "survey," you'll have ample opportunity to familiarize your charges with a few of the mechanics of verse, which knowledge can then be put to use later when they begin composing their own verse in composition. With junior high school students, I think the chronology should be the same, but their "survey" can deal with fewer of poetry's technical aspects. On the other hand, there is no reason why junior high school cannot be the level at which you use the more sophisticated approach. However, I have tried it both ways more than once, and each time came to the conclusion that my efforts with the latter approach resulted only in my eighth graders looking at me as if they were finally witnessing living proof of their suspicions—that I was an eccentric.

But then that is neither here nor there. What follows is the poetry-writing unit we are using now:

G—Poetry
1. Write a six-line rhyming poem (aa bb cc).
2. Write an eight-line, two-stanza poem (abba cddc).
3. Write a poem creating your own rhyme pattern.
4. Haiku.
5. Write at least five lines of free verse. (All assignments optional except #4.)

Although the poetry section appears chronologically to be the last five weeks of the course, it really is not. You implement it whenever you think your students are ready for it. And it need not be as tight, operationally, as it appears to be. If, for instance, you discover a student has begun something that is not precisely what the assignment calls for, I hardly think it would be catastrophic to allow him to pursue his own plan—especially since it just might turn out well. The specified end-rhyming patterns are really for those students who are not very poetry oriented and need some point at which to begin. Often a specific pattern is of help to them. If you are wondering about subject matter with respect to poetry-writing, sections "E" and "F" of the previous writing unit will serve very nicely.

Most of your students who choose to rush in where angels fear to tread will come up with pretty unspectacular verse, but a number of them each year will create pieces of poetry that represent a good deal more than dabbling. Take this schematic of word-ideas, for example, from a sensitive young lady in one of my recent third-hour classes:

Beat of Life

Sun beats, men toil,
  Bare backs, earthen hands.
    Planting, sowing, reaping harvests.

White shirt, black tie
  Phone rings, typewriter clicks
    Ringing, buzzing, whirling thoughts.

Machines pound, assembly lines,
　　Molten iron, orange, red, yellow.
　　　Pounding, throbbing, ear-splitting.

Dusting, sweeping, pick up toys,
　　Hauling newspapers, making lunch.
　　　Rustling, clattering, the house's beat.

Rows of books, dull eyes,
　　Drab desks, drab walls
　　　Numbers swim, verbs lie untouched, unwanted.

Work of life, beat of life.
　　Pounding, quiet, loving work,
　　　Rustling, clattering, ringing
　　　　Buzzing, screaming, crying.
　　　　　Work of life.
　　　　　Work.[6]

This, as you can see, was one of our human activities assignments—not poetry specifically, although at this stage of our program students are given the option on occasion. The class the above poem came from was given the option frequently. The reason, I think, is obvious; it was exceptionally talented.

You may be of the opinion that attempting to teach adolescents poetry-writing is something of an exercise in futility. If that is the case I would have to disagree. If you give your students some appreciation of the art form in the literature phase of your program, you are going to create the desire in many of them to at least have a go at it. In any event, whenever you assign the writing of poetry, you can always give an alternative prose assignment for those who give up easily.

And it should be understood that you need not be a poet yourself, or necessarily an authority on the subject in order to teach it effectively. Like me, I would guess most of you occasionally try your hand at writing it, and you have read and enjoyed reasonable amounts of it. But your understanding of what makes poetry poetry, and all of its nuances and complexities, is

---

[6] Pamela Marquardt is the authoress.

somewhat limited. But I'm not bashful; I try my hand at teaching it anyway. There is no reason I can think of why you should be fainthearted in this matter. And, as with me, you may even learn from your students something in the way of new dimensions connected with poetry forms.

However, there are fundamentals connected with poetry-writing, such as meter and of course rhyme (how about that), and the choice of poetic language (perhaps), and the mathematics of the thing—mood, voice, and so on. You can talk about the visual and audio forms that poems assume, whether they are free or metered verse, and about poetic license. And you can get pretty specific about techniques of description such as metaphor and simile. With respect to alliteration you come to discover that it is well to tread softly, lest your students overdo it. The word rhymes with obliteration, you know. Now, I doubt that you are going to get very far talking about poetic "feet" and "iambs," or firing such terms as "trochaic" and "dactylic" and "scansion" at students, at least before they have reached high school. And then I think the place to do it is ideally in the literature phase of your course. Most junior high school students, I have found, just aren't ready for an in-depth examination of the technical aspects of poetry. That doesn't necessarily mean that some of them aren't potential poets, however. Nor does it mean that talk of accented and unaccented syllables and metrical schemes will not make sense to them.

As for traveling from student to student during the times they are writing poetry, here you have to use judgment and tact to an even greater degree than when they are writing prose. Too much meddling can wreak havoc. May I suggest that at poetry time you settle into the practice of deskside visits only on the second day of their assignment—unless, of course, someone solicits your help. While your students are working themselves up into a poetic lather, they are going to put down all sorts of fantastic things on their papers which will tend to put you into a syntactical dither, especially if you make your visits too early in the assignment. But by the second day, it has been pretty well established what the finished product is going to be, if indeed there is going to be one at all. Then I think is the appropriate time for you to assume your "beat" up and down the aisles, offering help to individual students who seem to most need it.

Well, what do you look for? First of all, practically never free verse. When you find it, it is almost certainly going to be in an upper-track class—if you have the track system—or on the paper of an above-average student, nearly always female. Don't ask me why. All of this is based on experiences, and this has been one of them consistently over the years. Furthermore, when you happen onto a student who is composing free verse and knows it, it generally is good—assuming of course that one is qualified to judge whether free verse is good or bad. Quite possibly I am not. Since, therefore, free verse is virtually nonexistent among adolescent poets, you look for mostly the conventional kind of verse in your travels about the room. *And remember always that you are reading the material of adolescents.* Your subconscious is no place for that fact; you have got to keep it right smack in the front of your mind, otherwise you are going to want to suggest some very unrealistic alternatives to your students. Alternatives, which if implemented, are going to make the poetry not necessarily better, but most assuredly yours, not theirs. So if, for instance, you come upon something like this:

> Spring, the most beautiful time of the year,
> Is a season which all of us hold dear . . .

you have no grounds for suggesting alternatives. The student is doing well. He has a fair sense of rhythm, which should be a primary consideration, and he is following the pattern you laid out for him, assuming the assignment called for a rhyming couplet. The theme leaves something to be desired, but you have no cause to even suggest that to him. If you're looking for the Marianne Moore kind of thing, or some Dylan Thomas, or perhaps Eliot, you are going to be disappointed. Nor in your travels are you likely to discover any Tennysons, Whittiers, or Whitmans —hardly even a Guest. Just adolescents struggling with an experience they are quite probably ill-acquainted with. However, if you are confronted with a situation resembling this:

It was brisk and cold on a wintery night.
The trees were covered with sparkling snow bright.
The jingle of sleigh bells so loud and fair,
In hopes that St. Nicholas soon would be there . . .

you may strike, pointing out, I suppose, that the fourth line shatters the poem's continuity and perhaps even its coherency. I daresay an additional remark that the line has already been used would be in order, too, even though you might feel it hardly necessary to call attention to such an obvious fact. At the same time, you would, I think, suggest that the rest of the stanza has a pleasant meter and an effective rhyme, and tell the young writer to think of all the other words that could rhyme with "fair."

Most of the time, though, you are going to be suggesting revisions which will improve meter, lead students to a better choice of diction, aid them in giving their poems more attractive visual form, and get them out of syntactical binds. In short, the help you give your young poets is to a large extent the same kind you give them when they are writing prose.

Haiku

In the poetry part of the writing unit presented earlier, there is an assignment calling specifically for free verse, which it has already been pointed out, is as rare as economy in the Pentagon; hence, its optional status. You will notice it follows haiku, a marvelous little vehicle for acquainting young language students with some of the elements of free verse.

For those of you who are not familiar with it, haiku consists of 17 syllables of free verse in three lines of 5, 7, and 5 syllables, respectively. Its theme has to do with nature. To be genuine haiku, it may not relate merely to nature in general. Rather, it must relate to some specific event and it must be a "now" event; that is, a present-tense expression. I mention these things just for the record and hasten to add that your students and you don't always have to stick to all the rules.

With such a diminutive form, there has to be word economy, so one of the first things you point out in teaching haiku is to make every word count, and therefore select the best words possible. Whatever it is about haiku, though—the subject matter, its brevity, or its precise mathematical makeup—students "dig" it no matter what their level of achievement happens to be. A classroom visitor is always tipped off—when up and down the aisles he sees dozens of extended fingers tallying syllables—that he is witnessing a "haiku caper."

Even if you are unfamiliar with this literary form, a mere description of it is nearly as good as an introduction. Nonetheless, here is an example:

> The oriole's nest:
> Elementary, yet wondrous
> Product of instinct.

Some of my students in all probability would comment on the poor word-choice, even perhaps that "elementary" has five syllables and therefore makes the second line an eight- instead of seven-count unit. To which I would reply, "Elementary is one of those words which can have two different beat counts, depending on how many you want it to have in your haiku, isn't it, class? Say yes."

But when you are teaching haiku, you don't have to be all that conventional. You may even, if you wish, move the haiku form into other subject matter areas besides nature. Then, of course, it would no longer be haiku, I guess. But then French often ceases to be French when it reaches America. We take notorious liberties with all language forms, so why not with haiku? After all, we gave the Japanese democracy and they transformed it into a profitable enterprise.

You may expect in the course of one assignment of haiku anywhere from six to 20 or 25 creations from each student. My classes, I would guess, average about ten per student—with no sweat.

I think you can readily see why this assignment immediately precedes the one having to do with free verse. Moving from three lines to five in this literary form is a reasonably gentle sequential step, and if students can't take it, you always have the alternative of letting them work out more haiku. Significantly, I have never had a student who was afraid to try writing haiku, and most of them tackle the task with no little enthusiasm.

In a later chapter, you will see some recent examples of haiku from some of my past students. If by then you are not at least a little enthused about its possibilities as one useful ingredient in the enrichment of your language program, no harm done. God knows I tried, though.[7]

Revision Techniques

In composition, revision of rough and subsequent drafts in arriving at the best possible finished product is almost always a problem for students at any grade level, all the way to senior in college. We English teachers constantly talk about the desirability of more or less gradual evolution to the "final" draft, but we often do not furnish our students with specifics. Perhaps it is because many of us do not have them. A few summers ago, while doing graduate work at Wisconsin State University—Eau Claire, I came across an intriguing and valuable curriculum study, the result of extensive research done at the curriculum development center of the University of Nebraska and published in 1965. There was considerable material useful to the writing student *and* teacher in that study, but one little "formula" pertinent to our present discussion has proved practicable to me and I'm sure can be to you, if given enough stress in the classroom. It attacks draft revision systematically with the specifics one (at least this one) is looking for. The writer revises: (a) by elimination—removal of words, phrases, and clauses which clearly clutter or add nothing substantive; (b) by relocation—repositioning of words, phrases, and clauses (espe-

---

[7] For a brief but excellent introduction to haiku, see Henderson, Harold G., *Haiku in English,* Charles E. Tuttle Co.: Publishers, Rutland, Vermont and Tokyo, Japan, 1967.

cially modifiers); (c) by transformation—changing language structures from one grammatical form to another (including combination); (d) by addition—adding words, phrases, and clauses for tone, clarity, et cetera (imbedding).[8]

To see just how this might work, let's compose a hypothetical paragraph in "rough" draft form and then revise it, symbolizing the formula for demonstration purposes: **E** for elimination, **R** for relocation, **T** for transformation, **C** for combination, and **A** for addition.

                         E   **C**

The conductor (of the train) shouted the signal for departure;

                         R   **T**

Judy threw her mama (from the train) a kiss. (A gentle tug was

         R   **E**   **R**

felt by her) (as the engineer/of the train/eased forward on the

        E   **C**   **A**   **E**

throttle) (of the engine). The huge monster crawled (slowly) out

        A

of the station.

The symbols having indicated what can or must be done, we compose the next draft with the symbols still present to make it easier for the reader to follow what has been done:

                   E   **C**

The conductor shouted the signal for departure, and Judy threw

               R   **R**

her mama a kiss (from the train). (As the engineer eased forward

          E   **T**   **C**   **A**

on the throttle), (she felt a gentle tug), and the huge green and

A   **E**   **A**   **A**

yellow monster crawled out of the station, (creaking and groaning,

       A   **A**   **A**   **A**   **A**   **A**

the thunder of its diesel engine sending shudders through the

      A

station platform).

---

[8] *Syntax and the Rhetoric of the Sentence—Grade 9;* Experimental Materials; Nebraska Curriculum Development Center, The University of Nebraska, 1965—page 3.

First, "of the train" was eliminated because it was unnecessary in the context of the first sentence. Secondly, the comma splice in the second line was nullified by the use of "and" to combine its two parts. Thirdly, "from the train" was relocated for obvious reasons. Fourthly, lines three and four were transformed into active voice and combined with the last sentence. The prepositional phrases "of the train" and "of the engine" were eliminated as clutter, and the resultant, entirely new last sentence was further enhanced through the use of addition or imbedding.

This kind of thing is obviously practical only for demonstration purposes. We don't, of course, resort to labels while we're writing, but the application of the formula to discover some of the things that can go wrong with students' writing is made easier with some such example either dittoed for distribution or put on the board for a few weeks. I have found the latter practice the more effective of the two.

The principle of the thing is highly practical. You have a tool here which not only can help to organize your student's attack on his rough draft and all those following it, but likewise yours when you are giving him help. And it makes no difference what you look for first; whatever weakness is spotted is as good a starting point as any.

A cursory reading of what your student has so far written will usually reveal whether or not it contains clutter words or groups.

Needed repositioning very often manifests itself clearly in any writing, since it results in awkwardness and/or obvious lack of clarity.

The need for combination is harder to detect, but that too at times flies off the paper and hits you smack between the eyes.

Imbedding as a revision requires considerable explanation by you. It has to do primarily with the theory that one can never exhaust the possibilities of developing a thought. Of course, there is a stopping point for expansion if only just for efficiency's sake, but most students suffer from word thrift—and so with them the concept of imbedding has to be emphasized almost ad nauseam.

Revision by transformation—the need for it, that is—is the most elusive of the five. When do you suggest an indirect object in lieu of a prepositional phrase, or an appositive in lieu of a relative clause, or active in lieu of passive voice? Often a pronoun instead of a noun or a possessive instead of a phrase is as much as you will want to propose to some students. May I add that passive to active voice transformation is an excellent vehicle for pointing out the value of word economy and added clarity? You would do well to watch for every opportunity to suggest it, where it improves the student's writing, of course. To further help your classes in applying this technique, periodic revision of dittoed student paragraphs (preferably from the previous year) through class discussion, is certainly called for.

All of this talk about revision has brought us to perhaps as vital an activity as there exists in the whole process of language manipulation. That activity is proofreading. It is not only essential to good writing, it is possibly the most difficult concept to sell your students. Because of this, you must emphasize its importance with a vengeance—literally. Start by suggesting there really is no such thing as a final draft. Then talk about slow, careful reading and the necessity for assuming that your students are going to find mistakes in their copy. Next, try to develop in them the technique of mental listening while they read their copy—with an "ear" for run-ons, garbled passages, awkward constructions, ineffective fragments, et cetera. Finally, convince your students that two, or even three proofreadings are certainly not out of the question—if there is time. If you manage to develop good proofreading habits in your charges before the first semester is over, consider your efforts well-rewarded.

Your Role

Are you enthusiastic about your creative writing program? If you are, it is probably because you are convinced of its essential character in your language program. If you are not, chances are your students aren't either. Of course, the care with which you plan your writing program to begin with, certainly will reflect your attitude toward it. But your enthusiasm for it must show through—in you. And it will show through most apparently in the manner in which you assume your role as a catalyst hovering in the aisles, and as unassumingly as possible, but as frequently as necessary, aiding and abetting the cause:

> "John, do you suppose that sentence could be eliminated or perhaps put somewhere else in your paragraph?" "Valerie, why should this phrase be closer to the word 'men' in the line above it?" "Alison, read that second sentence and see if you think it makes sense." "Mark, who does 'they' in the middle of your paragraph refer to?" "Bruce, can you think of a more precise verb for 'move' in that last sentence?"

There are those who rarely need you and those who very much need you, but neither of the two groups is particularly anxious to have you "meddle"—early in the year, at any rate. So it is often by cajolery (or a change of mouthwash?) that you gain their confidence. That failing, you must take it by force if you are to be of any use at all. As the weeks go by, you find fewer and fewer students hiding their writing from you, and before the year is very far along, practically no one spurns your visits. However, too much interference can destroy spontaneity and sometimes cut off in its prime something that seemed to have promise.

You will discover also that the least said (by way of details) in assigning compositions, the better. I can't emphasize this too much. Never make your assignments so involved that they become intolerably channeled. A flexible assignment reaps its rewards in terms of imaginativeness in student writing. And why prescribe any specific length for your writing assignments? My stock answer for "How long should it be?" has been, "Oh, 5 foot 8, maybe 9." Beyond the third week of school, the question seldom if ever comes up again. During my academic career, whenever I have been asked to write—which is seldom—I cannot recall any of my instructors ever having given the assignment without adding the precise or approximate number of words it should be. Numbers of words in the context of creativity, I think, is another unnecessary invasion by the irrelevant. It is kind of like telling an artist to paint your portrait using only so many milligrams of each color. It is just another impediment—a stipulation which is not the artist's and therefore limits him in his creativity. There must, I suppose, be some stipulations in any writing assignment, but number of words is certainly not one of them.

If you make it clear to your students that in giving an assignment you mean exactly what you say—no more, no less—then your chances of being questioned incessantly from the floor are very remote indeed. Say, for instance, you ask for a composition on the human activity of eating, and nothing more. The word "composition" implicitly allows them to create anything from a one-paragraph assignment to a full-blown narrative with dialogue—or even poetry. The phrase "human activity of eating" tells them that this is an area of subject matter and allows for considerable flexibility of approach. It could deal, say, with a look at the table habits of a baby brother in the milieu of a paragraph; it might be a dialogue between a husband and wife at the breakfast table; it could be a poem about ants at a picnic. Once your writing program is well under way, the techniques of assigning that you use pose no problems from the standpoint of clarity if you have made your students understand that however much or little you say in giving one, you are to be taken literally. You will find the method not only conducive to creativity, but a valuable time-saver as well.

It may be an eccentricity of mine, but it seems to me if you are going to collect the creative effort of a student for appraisal, you should return it to him with appropriate markings and comments as soon as possible—like, for instance, the next day. Indeed, it is incumbent upon you to follow this practice, because if you use the staggered-schedule plan you will, before the day is out, receive another 30-plus batch of compositions to mull over. Fidelity to this kind of regimen is essential and in the long run, gratifying, for I am sure it creates a degree of enthusiasm in your writing program which would not otherwise be present. As a matter of fact, if for one reason or another you do not return a class's compositions the day after you collect them, there is noticeable restlessness in the room (conditioned reflex) and always someone to ask you if you are going to hand "those things we did yesterday" back to them. Somewhat the same reaction sets in if your students do not write on the appointed day. Students not only become accustomed to the practice of writing every week, they actually come to like it—believe me. And why shouldn't they? Why shouldn't students take pleasure in putting a little of themselves on paper once a week? Our only regret should be that we are unable to let them do it more frequently.

Every English teacher has his own set of marking symbols, but among them I should think there would be five universal symbols; namely, the **E, R, T, C,** and **A** in conjunction with the revision formula we discussed earlier. They clarify a great deal for the student with respect to the weaknesses of his writing, once he knows what they stand for and their significance in relation to composition.

And what can one English teacher say about written comments on the student's creation? Be as positive as possible? Yes. As kind as possible? Yes. As candid as possible? Yes. As brief as possible? Yes. As entertaining as possible? Yes. I hesitate to say more except this. Strangely enough, you will find it is the editorial comment the student reads first—all too frequently, excluding everything else you write on his returned paper. Why not use it as a vehicle for student vocabulary building, then? Thus, for example, a one-word comment, "Laconic," might just induce your young writer to look up the word—naturally, after he has first asked you what it means.

By the way, have you tried marking papers lately with something besides red pencil or pen? Would you believe it; my students prefer green. I polled them not long ago and green won out by quite a plurality. Red was near the bottom of the list. I asked them why. Here are some of the answers they gave: "It hurts my eyes." "That's the only color teachers ever use." "Red is for neckties." "It always looks like the teacher's cut himself."

So I use green. I must say it gives composition papers a much less garish appearance.

Do you require your students to keep all the compositions they have produced over the school year? What do you think of having them bind their creations in some kind of a folder and turning them in to you in June? It seems to me such a practice is a fitting climax to any comprehensive writing program. First, it is an excellent opportunity for your students to experience the satisfaction of seeing their efforts (35 to 40 compositions) for a whole year, compiled in good order within the confines of something fairly permanent. Second, it seems a legitimate extension of the idea that whatever they have to say about life is just as important as what the next guy has to say. Wouldn't it be something if this kind of anthology were kept by students at every grade level from first grade on up through high school? In giving this assignment, you can attach a few stipulations, if you wish, to give it added significance. You might require that they file their compositions in chronological order, for example. You could then perhaps add something about neatness and completeness. And finally, appeal to their pride of ownership by pointing out the exclusivity of such a possession; when you hand a composition assignment back, tell them to hang on to it with pride for posterity.

SUMMARY

1. This look into the written composition phase of your language program represents the first facet of what is essentially a student-oriented, language-learning course. The scope of the program, within its parts and as a whole, is possible only if the remedial measures suggested in Chapter 1 are implemented.

2. In language curriculum, a comprehensive written composition program is one of the most effective and financially realistic means to curriculum enrichment that education has. Aside from its complete economic feasibility, it allows students to satisfy their innate desire for self-expression, and in the process gives them

just that much more self-knowledge and ability to use their language effectively. In addition, it makes possible your real function as an English teacher, in that it allows for development of both dimensions of communicating in your students. Furthermore, it is an effective way to slow down the process of depersonalization in today's education: a comprehensive writing program establishes a highly personal relationship between you and your students.

3. A comprehensive writing program can be a reality in your classroom if you abandon the trivia in your teaching, adopt some method (the staggered schedule being one example) to soften the impact of large classes, and supplement the guide with your own ideas of what a good writing program should include.

4. In the teaching of writing, a most realistic starting point would seem to be single-paragraph development, beginning with descriptive techniques and moving along through expository and persuasive writing. The number of single-paragraph assignments may be reduced as students advance from grade to grade, but some single-paragraph development should be done in all the grades.

5. Narrative writing is best taught in conjunction with dialogue and beyond the single-paragraph form. In teaching narrative writing it is important to stress proper punctuation, particularly dialogue punctuation, and techniques which lead to a credible tone in your students' narrative.

6. With the completion of the single-paragraph and narrative-with-dialogue phases of your writing program, your students are ready in varying degrees to grapple with composition assignments which include elements of what they have learned thus far. The rest of your program should be a mixture of single-paragraph and multi-paragraph (with and without dialogue) compositions.

7. The teaching of poetry can begin with the poetry-survey phase of your literature course. Students should be given almost complete freedom in the writing of poetry. For those who are not able to cope with it, an optional prose assignment must always be available.

8. The Japanese literary form of haiku is an excellent aid in the teaching of free-verse writing.

9. A successful writing program must have your enthusiasm behind it. A well-organized, constantly changing, flexible writing unit is certainly one manifestation of that enthusiasm, but your attention to the individual needs of your students while they are writing is the strongest manifestation of it—that and your prompt correcting and evaluating of each student's composition.

10. Assign compositions with as little talk as possible.

11. With your deskside visits, there is ample opportunity to teach on a one-to-one basis the fundamentals of syntax; this is the most opportune time to teach it.

12. Revision of composition can be systematic. Fundamentally, one revises by elimination, relocation, transformation, combination, and addition. In marking papers, use of the revision symbols is helpful to your students in discovering what is wrong with their writing.

3

Organizing and Implementing an Effective Oral Composition Program

---

The importance of oral composition can only be considered with reference to the whole of active communicating. If communication is vital in the educative process generally, and in language learning specifically, then oral composition must carry as much weight as written composition. Communicating is communicating whether you are writing or speaking, and the latter activity has to be considered just as vital, and therefore taught just as emphatically as the former. Both facets of the skill are called for in light to today's "gaps," all of which are in essence communications gaps. If we are to keep in touch, both facets need developing.

The apparent neglect (past and present) of both in public school education, it seems to me, constitutes a "conspiracy" which I think has played a significant role in rendering America virtually incommunicado domestically and internationally. The ability of the leadership of this nation to communicate with force, understanding, candor, and lucidity, at the very least leaves something to be desired. Our religious leaders are discovering to their dismay that they have been virtually incommunicado with the masses. You need only watch the charadery of election campaigning to know the chasm that lies between us and our political leaders. The violent confrontations between students and administrations in the intellectual community should be ample evidence of another incredible gap. A preponderance of the advertising and programing you see on television just has to tell you something about the communicating abilities of the business and entertainment segments of our society. We apparently are not reaching one another. It isn't as if we weren't trying to keep in touch. There is an unconscionable amount of scribbling and mouthing going on in America today. That is what makes the whole scene so unedifying and tragic.

There is no lack of need, then, for the *effective* communicator in America—and to be an effective communicator, one needs both facets of the skill of active communicating. Oral composition happens to be one of them. But aside from the nation's need, there is your need as a teacher for vocal idea exchange among your students, if for no other reason than to charge the atmosphere of your classroom, thereby making education just that much less stuffy and relentless for you and your students. I can think of no other activity that so brightens the academic environment.

Finally, and most important, there is a need in every student to satisfy his innate desire for self-expression. While creating on paper satisfies part of that need, creating on stage can be no less important, and may well be more so, for when he is on stage he, as well as his product, are on display.

Yet, so seldom do our students stand before their peers and expound on the problems of our time, that I sometimes wonder if there is a Supreme Court ruling I haven't yet heard about. One reason, of course, is that crowded curriculums and classrooms make frequent presentations impractical, if not impossible.

You and your students (as I and mine do) I would guess indulge in give-and-take class discussions more or less spontaneously, but if you set aside one day at least every other week in your schedule for formal presentations, and in addition require an oral book report of your students every four or five weeks, you in effect guarantee each of them about 20-plus experiences before an audience in the course of an academic year. That is not nearly frequent enough, but with the staggered schedule it is relatively easy to make an adjustment, which for a time would allow for weekly oral presentations simply by eliminating the free reading period for two or three weeks at a time. So, in effect, by using your own best judgment in manipulating the staggered schedule, you can add significantly to the scope of your oral composition program. Whatever you choose to do, with each succeeding presentation, I'm sure you will become convinced of the efficacy of this kind of program, for it is in "doing their thing" in front of the class that your students will manifest more consistent improvement than in any other phase of their language activities. Just in terms of the self-confidence and poise they gain, a program of this nature is well worth pursuing.

Techniques: The Oral Book Report

If your students present their book reports orally, using the summary approach, I can guess the experience every four or five weeks becomes something of an exercise in anticlimax. Thirty or 35 oral summaries in the course of a class period or two tend to have a mesmerizing effect on audiences.

But it isn't as if a summary were the only kind of information students could present about the books they have read. In fiction, for example, there are always any number of intriguing characters whose traits and physical attributes can be described. Explanation of the title of the book relative to its plot can be entertaining, particularly if a student offers his own interpretation. Why a book was good or bad presents an opportunity for some interesting reporting, at least by the kind of students who are intellectually able to recognize why. "Which character, next to the hero or heroine, was most important to the story?" "Why?" are two questions, the answers to which can serve very well as another kind of book report. Is there any reason why your students can't relate a few facts about the author instead of or in addition to the book? With respect to reports on biography and autobiography, many of the same possibilities hold true. And with other kinds of nonfiction where summary seems the only "out," there is no reason why a student's report cannot take the form of a summary.

Now, since your classes are large, limit each student to about a minute per report, and you stand a good chance of completing the entire project in a period's time with perhaps a carry-over of a few students to a later date. A minute seems hardly worth the effort, I know, but with proper organization prior to his report, a student can say a great deal about a character in fiction, or about an author, or why the book he read was dull or entertaining, or how the title relates to the plot. A minute is ample time for a summary too. May I remind you that most television commercials are a minute in length?

You don't have to be hard-nosed about the time element, however. Say a student slops over in his report by 15 or 30 seconds, there is no reason to panic, but if you make it clear that book reports are to be somewhere between say, 45 seconds and a minute and a half in length, very few of your students will find it troublesome to abide by the rule—especially if they have organized their presentations carefully. From the standpoint of organization the exercise turns out to be a valuable lesson in mental discipline.

The Student-Oriented Discussion

The book report, though minor, plays a useful role in your oral composition program, for it gives your students brief periodic experiences before an audience. It is a valuable supplement, then, to the major thrust of your program, the student-led discussion. *The principle of this technique centers around your role as a listener.*

Every student not only makes an oral presentation; he also leads any discussion which may follow it, contributions from the audience ideally coming as the result of a raised hand. You can expect him to do a good job if you make it known to him that he can rebut if he feels the need to, or simply listen to whatever comment comes from the floor and then call on some other student; in other words, if you make his job as easy as possible for him.

It will take your classes some time to adjust to the idea of one person at a time having the floor, but stick with it. Improvement, though gradual, will be steady. Naturally there will be times when a discussion gets out of hand, and then a bang of the hand on your desk top is a reasonable expedient for restoring order. But there are limits to what a hand can do. That is to say, one or two bangs on the desk is about it for one period. After that the act approaches meaninglessness. It is also painful. In the long run, mastery of this situation by the participants comes with experience, but a husky-voiced, heavy-handed catalyst helps.

You are going to discover, too, how really immature some of these discussions can be. That is to be expected and you cannot very well judge them by adult standards. During a particularly "bad" performance, you may decide to interject an idea of your own if only to give the thing a shot in the arm. That is your prerogative, and sometimes it turns out to be just the needed ingredient. Just as often, however, it results in a noticeable deceleration in the discussion, if not total silence. Students themselves will usually succeed in spanning any valleys among the peaks if left on their own. With your lower track classes you may expect (but won't necessarily always get) somewhat immature discussions. But discussion is not usually immature to those who engage in it, and that should be of primary importance to you. *The fact that there is idea exchange going on at all should override every other consideration.*

There will be varying degrees of discussion with each presentation. When the discussion is high-spirited, protracted, it is unusual that more than six students get to the front of the room. Some days more than that make the trip; on other days, as few as one. Recently this happened as the result of a student's rather provocative presentation on Christianity. The setting was in one of my upper track classes and I uttered not one word during the entire discussion. Indeed, I had no desire to. The performance was so out of the ordinary and intriguing that I could only sit and listen. Such things as the allegorical nature of the Old Testament, Christ as the enemy of the establishment, evolution and the Bible, the scandal of divided Christians, and the non-involvement of institutionalized Christianity, were brought up. I remember one comment by a diminutive but unusually mature young fellow to the effect that we glory in looking down our noses at the ancients and all their "silly gods," and at the "fat Buddha," while subscribing to such doctrines as that of "the devil, a white-bearded Supreme Being, and even immortality," as long as it is on Christian terms. The bell rang much too soon and I was still sitting in one of the student desks when my next class arrived.

To give more students a chance to lead discussion, you will need to set some kind of a time limit, which is what I should have done on the day in question. But you find that a bit difficult to do at times. It really becomes a matter of value judgment: Will the maximum number of students benefit by one long cogent discussion, or several shorter ones, some of which might be anything but? There are other factors governing the number of presentations in a given period, of course. The effectiveness of delivery is one. Differences in class temperament is another. And I suppose even such things as barometric pressure and room temperature have something to do with it.

You will experience hours of pleasure with these discussions, and your pleasure will come primarily from the realization that one of your students is really and truly conducting the class through a discussion without any comment from you—unless you find it absolutely necessary to inject yourself into the affair. There is an added pleasure, as time goes by, in observing your students' reactions to the reality of discussions that belong exclusively to them.

A Resource Unit

You can set up a resource unit in oral composition just as in written composition. Here, as in your writing unit, simplicity is the key to success. Even with senior high school students, requiring too complicated a report is, I think, going to prove self-defeating. If you make it a point to deal with subject matter which can be researched rather easily, your students are not so apt to become discouraged. Really, the prime goal of this phase of your language course is to give adolescents practice in speaking before an audience, with any research they do—library or otherwise—necessarily occupying a secondary position. I think if you pick broad categories and pursue them in round-robin style, your program has a good chance for variety. It also will have flexibility, allowing maximum opportunity for students to accomplish the task at hand using one of several choices of approach. How about these categories, for instance?—People; school life; civil rights; religion; local politics; the military; higher education; the drug problem; national politics; and conservation.

Generally under the category of "people" you may set up discussions dealing with national figures, but this need not be a foregone conclusion. A local personage (Milwaukee's mayor, for example) surrounded by some controversy, can spark as much discussion as one who has greater national significance. "Higher education" could include everything from a talk which deals with the "necessity" for a degree in today's society to one which contains commentary, based on some modest research, on the S. D. S. Under "conservation" there could be talks about nationalizing state parks (currently a hot topic in our state), pollution, or municipal water shortages. Discussion of religion I think is sadly neglected in education. The old adage about it and politics being subjects which are best avoided is invalid. Of all the discussions my classes have had bearing on religion, there has never been one which descended to the level of invective or anything approaching it. Indeed, I find a great deal more mutual respect among most young people regarding individual beliefs than among some of my adult acquaintances. Shunning a subject which represents such an inherent part of all societies—our own included—seems to me the height of folly. Religion (whether you have it or not) is an integral part of the real world. As for politics, what subject could be more vital to man the political animal? I classify as hogwash those claims that it belongs in the social studies, not the English classroom. Why not in both? How can you departmentalize any kind of idea exchange? Besides, the two subjects present opportunities positively pregnant with vitality, and virtually guarantee vibrant discussion among youth. A talk on ecumenism to an audience of Catholic and Protestant students will usually generate enough discussion among average or above-average groups to last an entire period. Give your students an assignment built around the subject of communism and the results are roughly the same.

Another workable unit could be one which is strictly magazine-oriented. Assign students detailed card-noted summary reports of magazine articles pertinent to somewhat more specific subject areas such as the following: automobiles, space, world hunger, ESP, war, the cinema, skin diving, pro-football, pro-basketball, hockey, collegiate football, collegiate basketball, racing, golf, animals, astrology, astronomy, television, poverty, art, books, the theater, air travel, women's fashions, men's fashions, the population explosion, railroads, meteorology, radio, highway safety, agriculture, the U. N. A second part of the report could be the student's reaction to the article, the entire report followed by the same kind of student-oriented discussion referred to above. The latter unit allows for a more flexible approach than the former. For example, you can assign each student in a class a different subject area, thereby covering many areas in one assignment. Or you can assign all your students the same subject area, thereby covering one area per assignment. And five or six groups reporting on as many different subject areas is just as feasible. It all depends on how much variety of subject matter you want over a given assignment, and any one of the three schemes is suitable for this kind of oral composition program. We have used all of the approaches in my classes and the relative merits of each balance out pretty evenly. In all honesty I must admit, however, that I (and I think my students) favor the first plan over the latter two.

Well, let's assume you have the first kind of the above resource units developed; that is, the round robin unit beginning with the broad category of "people." For your initial project you could assign each of your students a talk on some individual who is prominent in one or another phase of national life, plus a report on a magazine article by him, about him, or connected with his field of endeavor. There need be no duplication of assignments within any one class, since it is easily possible to cull some library reference source such as *Current Biography* for as many different people as you have students. As for the matter of magazine articles, *The Reader's Guide* very ably solves any problems students may meet in locating suitable subject matter. In this phase of your program you can plan on perhaps an average of ten students presenting their talks in a period's time, since any discussion which ensues consists mostly of questions and answers about the subjects of the talks. However, occasionally something of a more controversial nature from a magazine article may add length to the discussion. From a sequential standpoint "people" is the most logical topic to begin your academic year. Because it produces for the most part this kind of subdued question and answer discussion, it breaks your students in gently to the task of leading their classmates in idea exchange from the front of the room. At ten presentations a week, then, every other week (or for a time, every week, if you wish), this first category in your unit would take about three class sessions or three to six weeks to complete, depending on how you manipulate your staggered schedule. As you get into the other general subject areas, discussion periods following each talk increase in vitality and length, requiring you to set a time limit on them. A time span of five minutes of discussion after each talk seems realistic where students number up to 30 or 35 in a class. However, relatively few of their discussions will last that long.

How might you assign talks dealing with a general category such as "school life"? Well, again there seems nothing wrong with making the assignments as simple as possible. Gentle, sequential steps, remember. Start out by asking one row of students to prepare individual talks about why they think the school's dress and grooming code is or is not a good thing from the student's standpoint. Another row could prepare a commentary on the school's hot lunch program. Give a third row some such title as "How Much Power Should the Student Council Have?" Another, "How Much Power Does the Student Council Have?" And so forth, following roughly the same procedure for each general category. With regard to the latter two categories, as part of their reports encourage students to interview teachers, administrators, and other students for their views, using, wherever possible, direct quotations. It is virtually a certainty that you are not going to get through the entire list of general categories before the end of the year, but if you do, then go back to the top of the list and begin all over with "people," compiling another list of prominents on the national and international scene.

Perhaps you don't want to always give oral composition assignments as early as a week or two weeks before they are to be presented. There is no reason why the time allowed for preparation of material cannot be as little as 20 minutes if you wish. Some students, given a quarter hour or so to scribble a few notes for use in presenting their views on a current topic, can come up with some pretty effective commentary. As a matter of fact, the one mentioned above that had to do with Christianity, was just such a presentation.

Certainly worthy of mention is the library experience this kind of resource unit can give your students. *The Reader's Guide* and *Current Biography,* to mention just two reference sources, are especially useful. For many of the categories of your unit, the former source has significant value to students because of its subject-oriented structure. And specifically, for the "people" category, the latter is ideal. Beginning at the junior high school level, I think students are pretty much aware of what reference sources there are in any library, but an explanation by you is in order, just in case. In our system, a three-day library orientation course early in the year theoretically solves many of the problems students may have in this regard.

I see no reason why implementing these kinds of oral composition units at the high school level need be any more complicated than at the junior high school level. The same goals are relevant in both environments: (1) to give students practice in basic researching and consolidating their material into card-note form, (2) to increase their confidence and poise before a group, (3) to further satisfy their inherent desire for self-expression, and (4) to liven up the academic atmosphere.

I mentioned earlier that it is in this facet of your language program that you will be able to detect tangible results, more so than in any other part of your program. I find it simply astonishing the way students work at correcting themselves when they are performing in the presence of their peers. And yet, I guess it is not so astonishing after all. If you give adolescents frequent, regular, specific tasks in this area, and make the task simple enough, yet meaningful, they will recognize the goals of such a program without your having to spell them out. They want to be more articulate; they want to learn new skills; they want to overcome their shyness; they want to express themselves; they want a livelier classroom.

Evaluating Student Performance

May I be painfully elementary by suggesting that you divide the oral presentation task into three distinct areas: posture, delivery, and content, and comment in each area specifically, using something in the nature of the following form?

I think you can easily see that this kind of evaluating device is in for constant revision of one sort or another. Indeed, you will find it necessary to revise it in some way every time you ditto a fresh supply. Lately, with the trends in dress and grooming, I have had to add the comment "Hair in eyes," but my students claim that's where hair belongs. It is difficult to with-

POSTURE	DELIVERY	CONTENT
Swaying	More volume	Organization weak
Shifting weight	Expressionless	Too little
Fidgety	Too fast	Too much
Nervous feet	Enunciation weak	Vague
Nervous hands	Conjunctionitis	Incoherent
Hands at sides, please	Continuity weak	
Feet closer together	Too dependent on notes	
A bit stiff	Poor choice of words	
Hair in eyes	Look at aud__ Oftener__ Scan audience	
Outstanding	Volume good	Well-organized
Good	Good audience contact	Interesting
Otherwise, good	Effective use of notes	Creative
	Discussion conducted well	

stand such devastating logic. However, the more detail (within reason) you can put on the form, the better. Each class has its own peculiar bad habits, but most of the descriptions on the above form apply to virtually all students in the secondary grades. Obviously you have to develop and continuously revise a form that adapts to your classes.

Posture

By the end of the first quarter of your program I think the vast majority of posture problems among your students will be cleared up, or as one sharp student of mine put it: "We've been posturized." Early in the program there is much shifting of weight or steady pressure on one leg, nervous arm and hand movements, swaying (either sideways or forward and backward), and just plain fidgetiness. But repeated evidence of weaknesses on the evaluation slips and added student experience soon bring about a noticeable decline in the vast majority of posture faults. It is helpful periodically to emphasize posture strengths vocally, however, and demonstrate, explaining such things as gesturing and occasional changes of position, and "at-your-sides" as the base position of their hands: "You were born with them there, so why not let well enough alone?" There is a tendency all through their presentations in some students to plant feet tight up against each other and stand much as a marine sergeant at attention, and at the other extreme to stand, feet wide apart, like a colossus. Striking a happy medium between the two extremes can only be effected demonstratively. Perhaps "only" is too strong, but I always ultimately resort to the demonstration, my descriptions of "a happy medium" having failed abysmally.

The further you progress in your program, the more often you are going to be able to check "Outstanding" and "Good" in the Posture column. A third item, "Otherwise, good," helps build confidence in the student, particularly early in your program. Theoretically, it could be checked even if as many as three or four weaknesses in posture had been checked above it. As with all positive comments, these three effect added assurance in the recipient, and once most of their posture problems have disappeared, one or another of these notations checked seems to result in an even better performance next time. There is undoubtedly one "fault" none of your students are going to manifest during their presentations, and that is overconfidence. So whenever the opportunity to check a positive comment under any of the columns presents itself, why not take advantage of it? For example, "Interesting," in the Content column could nearly always be checked whether you thought a student's presentation was or was not. It is probable he thought it was and quite possible his peers did. You are the best judge of when this kind of opportunity has arrived, however, remembering always that you are dealing with adolescents.

Of course, at the outset of your oral composition program it is important that you explain exactly what is meant by each of the terms in all three columns of the check sheet, even though it would seem that most of them are self-evident.

Conjunctionitis

There remain other unsolved and more serious problems considerably less facile of solution than those having to do with posture. Nearly all student oral presentations suffer from some kind of conjunctionitis, as you well know. The er-ah-and-uh syndrome is a familiar one. As a disc-jockey years ago, I came across a phenomenon in the radio business which unfortunately still seems to be extant: Dead air is tantamount to trauma among radio personnel. "If you don't know what you're going to say next, say anything," seems to be the going dictum. On my programs I had an anti-dead-air gimmick called "Alfred." Alfred was my alter-ego, a weird, scratchy, unoriginal old-timer voice. Every time I found myself at a loss for words, I brought Alfred in, the psychology being that if something stupid came from Alfred's mouth, I at least would not be held accountable by the listening audience. The fact is, though, that dead air in small doses during any oral presentation is often quite effective, if only as an attention-getter. There is nothing quite like a noticeable span of silence in a sermon, for instance, to wake one up. So one reasonably effective cure I have used for the er-ah-and-uh malady is a short blurb every now and then about the advantages of dead air over useless and often irritating fill-ins when one is not sure at the moment what he is going to say next. Proper organization of the presentation is probably the best medicine for it, but if you tell a student that silent pauses now and then are not to be frowned upon as weaknesses in delivery, and on the contrary, can occasionally add strength to it, you make a point that I think most of them can understand.

As for the matter of organization of material before presentation, I doubt you can put too much emphasis on it for adolescents. To help assure pre-delivery organization, student familiarity with the card-notes method is indispensable. Don't suggest they get and use index cards—insist on it. Then show them how to use them. A chalkboard demonstration illustrating a hypothetical presentation in note form is a must, since you have to assume most of your students are not familiar with the technique—a reasonably correct assumption, by the way. Present your case for card-notes in simple terms, bearing in mind that your students may or may not choose to follow your specific plan or plans. My approach simply stated is eclectic. I give my students alternatives: (1) Outline your material on whatever number of cards you require for your presentation, dividing the subject matter where division points are most obvious. Under each division note salient points. (2) Simply jot down in your own words reminders as to where you are in your talk and what points you are going to make at each location. (3) Record your presentation word for word. Remember, however, that this technique tries your skill in maintaining eye contact with the audience considerably more than the other two plans.

I find that considerable numbers of students adopt the lattermost plan and with continued practice the vast majority of them succeed with it. Follow this procedure periodically at least for a good share of the first semester. There is the alternative of memorization, which you find rather large numbers of students wish to resort to. However they organize their material prior to presentation, the important thing is that they organize. If they do not, of course, their presentations are virtually doomed to failure from the outset.

The Speed Talker

Excessive speed in the delivery of oral presentations is another almost universal weakness of adolescents. Here again, demonstration is about as effective as anything if you want to make your point. Stopping the student early in his presentation and telling him to slow down sometimes works, but if he returns to the same rate of delivery (which is frequently the case) another interruption is hardly in order. Some kind of a hand signal from you, indicating that he should decelerate, proves to be the most effective remedy. With a good share of your students, however, hurried speech becomes less and less a problem as they find themselves more at ease in front of the class.

Expression

How do you get students to emote, even just a little, when they are doing this kind of thing? A check after "expressionless" on the sheet doesn't have much effect the first few times because students are usually too conscious of posture faults to be worried about any kind of "divertissement" during their talks. But as soon as a student's confidence begins to rise, you notice the first faint signs of improvement. A real monotone will often stress at unnatural places in his attempts to get some feeling into what he is saying. The effect is strange to the ears, but at least it is a signal that he is trying to overcome the fault and that you should perhaps leave well enough alone. But there are the many (not necessarily monotones) who never seem to say anything with that tone of conviction in their voices that is so necessary to get the attention of their audience and hold it. They may conquer most of their other oratorical vices, but it seems impossible for them to sound the least bit interested in what they are saying. Without a doubt, demonstration by you is the kind of technique that does the most good in these cases. But you have to be careful not to "ham it up." Show them rather where in a talk it is important to perhaps raise voice pitch, or pause to let an important point register, or slow down speech for maximum effect, or use hand-gesturing at strategic moments in a talk, et cetera. May I suggest the "Gettysburg Address" as an adequate vehicle?

You may also want to make a comment to students when they come back to get their evaluation slips: "Kerry, can't you get more oomph in your delivery?" or "Maureen, you sounded bored with your talk. Were you?" Bluntness can have its good effects too: "Lynn, what were you all choked up about?" As the names imply, the problem is most frequently found in the female of the species.

Continuity Weak

The notation "Continuity weak" often is really a suggestion that there was poor organization prior to presentation. If the item is checked, it is frequently a foregone conclusion that "Organization weak" under Content is also going to be checked. It is not unlikely that in addition the adjective "Incoherent" in the same column will get a check. That is why it is so important that you give your students rather detailed instruction in preparing card-notes; proper preparation is the key to effective oral presentation.

There are other causes for discontinuity, however. For example, there is the "friend" in the audience who is going through various and sundry facial gyrations, et cetera, in order to break the speaker up—and succeeding all too well. The problem, I think you will find, is most effectively dealt with by evicting the culprit from the room or sequestering him in your closet until his victim has finished what he is doing in the front of the room. It usually works—unless the victim has reached a state of absolute hysteria and is bent over, holding his stomach, red-faced, and appears to be on the verge of retching. Compassion, and sometimes sheer fright, guides you from this point and you tell him to be seated. If, however, you catch the culprit's act before it has gone too far, his victim generally recovers his aplomb and manages to complete his presentation without further trouble.

Another reason for discontinuity is a student's completely forgetting the next line in a memorized presentation, which could be the result of inadequate preparation or just nervous panic. An experience like this should prompt you to advise the individual to bring card-notes up front with him next time—even if he thinks he has memorized his material.

Diction

It is sometimes very difficult to decide whether a student has been guilty of poor word choice or not. The generation gap figures in here. What may be a totally meaningless word or phrase to you and me, may quite likely be precise and meaningful to our students. What you watch for mostly are expressions like, "She was hungry and tired *n' everything*," and such redundancies as in the repetition of the clause, "It tells about . . ." in reference to a book the student is reporting on. Then there are terms like "stuff" used as a noun, as in the expression, "that kinda stuff," and many more. Curiously enough, students seldom if ever use "ain't" anymore. Do you suppose we have worn it out with overuse as we have such words as "terrific," "excellent," "nice," "et cetera," et cetera?

Enunciation

Relatively few students have chronic enunciation problems. You have to be diplomatic here, particularly if you teach in an affluent community where parents have the wherewithal to spend a cool grand or two to have their youngsters' teeth straightened. Of course, I refer to braces, which may or may not create enunciation problems for a student. They usually do, I have found, to at least some degree, and so you can hardly check "Enunciation weak" in cases like this. Nor, obviously, in cases where there is a speech impediment. The kind of enunciation problem which I referred to as chronic is much more serious. So serious, in fact, that if you stop the student whose delivery is totally ineffective and virtually indecipherable because of it, you usually get an indecipherable answer to your question, "Can't you speak more clearly, Gary?" The best remedy seems to be occasional instruction after school on a one-to-one basis with the student. Lock your door, though; it will give your pupil a measure of confidence while he is practicing with you. There is nothing that so completely mortifies an adolescent as the sudden barging in of a peer while he is in session with his English teacher. The kind of problem this particular student has often stems from shyness anyway.

Volume

The delivery problem which seems to get solved the least number of times has to do with volume; that is, the lack of it.

The exhortation that "Your talk isn't going to generate very much discussion if we can't hear it" is only modestly successful in producing added volume. And demonstrations by you will, as in my case, quite possibly be met with some such remark as, "It's easy for you, you just naturally talk loud." But, as in so many other cases, the demonstration proves to be the most effective technique. Repeated checks of the "More volume" notation on a student's evaluation also have their effect.

There are some students whose decibel output is just incredibly small, and whatever cajoling or demonstrating or ear-cupping you engage in by way of remedy may seem like exercises in futility, but they all play their part in correcting the problem. As a last resort, simply interrupting the speaker with, "Okay, Julie, you may begin," sometimes does the trick amazingly well. With the soft talker you are going to have to exercise monumental patience.

Audience Contact

Another vexing problem, lying also in the area of delivery, has to do with audience contact—that is, getting the speaker to let the audience know that he knows they are out there by looking at them—ultimately, it is hoped, acquiring the scanning technique. A student can achieve "Good audience contact" without scanning, and you should always check that notation for any who do. But if he has not used that effective and all-inclusive sweep of the head and eyes back and forth over his audience, then a check after "Scan audience" is certainly also in order. Your students will pick up this mannerism only gradually, and as with all the rest, it requires perseverance on your part in insisting upon it, and on theirs in making a real effort to remember it with each of their presentations. Occasional demonstrations can help students to acquire this technique, and if you are a scanner during your "lectures," it follows that at least a portion of your students will pick up the habit by your example.

Signalling

From your position in the back of the room, it is helpful to use signalling techniques as the speaker progresses, to indicate what he should be doing that he is not doing, and vice versa. The technique is more effective, I think, if you are standing, but certainly does not require that you do so. The important thing is that your students understand what the signals mean and that you give them as unostentatiously as possible. The signal for more volume, for example, could be cupping your hand behind your ear (creative, huh?) ; for better audience contact, perhaps a touch of the thumb and forefinger to your eyelids; for less speed, a slow horizontal motion of the hand; for clearer enunciation, the formation of an "O" with thumb and forefinger. Bear in mind that too much signalling and too many different signals obviously can confuse the speaker. It would seem, then, that four critical signals or so serves the purpose.

Now, early in the year when you and your students are just beginning the oral composition part of your program, you are at times going to feel like a fool sitting there in the back of the room looking for all the world like a mental case—especially if you are trying to get through to a student who has many problems with oral presentation. Moreover, your students are apt to pay considerably more attention to your antics than you will want them to, but the novelty of your silent monologue wears off very quickly. If at the outset you remind your classes firmly that the front of the room is where the important action is, they soon stop glancing back at you to see what's coming next. In any event, the signalling system can be very useful in effecting improvement in your students' oral presentations. As a matter of fact, I have come to regard it as indispensable.

Too Dependent on Notes

When your students are working from notes, the tendency naturally is to over-depend on them, especially if they are not notes at all, but the presentation itself, word for word. Even with repeated chalkboard demonstrations of how to set up a talk in card-note form—dividing it up into its logical parts, giving each part a significant heading, putting those headings on cards, et cetera—you have students who insist on putting their entire presentation on the cards. If the presentation is not memorized, then the student giving it is going to be extremely dependent on his cards, and more than likely will have to read his presentation in its entirety. There are many who are able to do this and still maintain good visual contact with their audience, and you really have no cause for concern over them. But there are some who simply bury their heads in their cards and read on, oblivious of the audience. You have a reasonably "sure cure" for this kind of problem. Simply require them to prepare another report for the next session, re-emphasizing the card-notes technique, and offering them help if they need it.

Too Little or Too Much

These two comments in the Content column mostly apply to the student's oral book report, but a check after one or the other certainly can be occasionally called for in any kind of report. I hasten to add that a student's presenting too much material in the delivery of any report other than the book report is extremely rare.

Playback

My trusty little cassette tape recorder is proving to be worth every penny I paid for it. Used periodically in recording student-led discussions, it becomes a kind of electronic catalyst for group therapy at playback time. Now, I know some educators are going to take exception to the whole idea of collective electronic evaluation, but I use the technique for the following reasons: (1) kids from 5 to 95 enjoy listening to themselves and their peers on tape, and (2) they often profit by what they hear in terms of self-improvement. There is no comment from either the students themselves or me during the playback—unless one or another member of the class raises his hand signifying a desire to make a remark or ask a question. We simply listen to the tape and let it go at that. Before playback I ask my students to check the audio faults scored on their evaluation sheets against what they hear when they themselves are on playback. You may use the technique from the very beginning of your oral composition program if you wish. I think to be fair, though, this kind of self-evaluating device is better implemented during the second semester at the earliest, at which time the preponderance of your students will feel more like old pros at the game and hence, not in the least embarrassed at the prospect of having their presentations "aired."

Making an Evaluation

I suppose you are wondering about problems with respect to your actually marking the evaluation forms for oral composition. There is really nothing to it. You are going to have to be intent, though, on what a student is saying and doing while he is up in the front of the room. With practice—and you will get plenty of it—you will soon become a past master of the technique. One thing, however, you have to watch for is mid-talk corrections of either posture or delivery faults. For example, a student may begin his presentation shifting his weight from one leg to the other, and shortly afterwards become aware of the fault and correct it. Or his volume may be too low, and catching a signal from you, he may increase it. It is a good idea, in anticipation of this kind of thing happening, for you to wait a few seconds or perhaps up to a minute, depending on the length of the presentation, before you start checking the sheet.

I need hardly point out the need for your enthusiasm with respect to any oral composition program you pursue. Oral composition is certainly no less important than writing, and as such calls for the same kind of diligent attention from you. This includes the giving of help to individual students whenever they need it, and faithfully evaluating in writing each and every student performance. Enthusiasm in this phase of active communicating, I think, comes easier for both you and your students, simply because of its nature. As the subject matter pursued becomes increasingly provocative, leading to spirited class discussion, élan is more or less spontaneous.

One More Thing

There is probably not an English teacher reading this who at one time or another has not carried on activities in his classroom similar to those described above. The point is that *it has not been done consistently and relentlessly year after year in our public schools.* It is seldom if ever explicit curriculum, and very often it is merely extra-curricular. But what if it were? What kind of individual might come from a system which put into practice the kind of composition programs we have been discussing in Chapters 2 and 3—in all the grades? Since it is doubtful such a school system exists, we have nothing tangible on which to base an answer to the question. But even if we hypothesize such a system, it would at the very least produce:

A young adult who has dealt with language manipulation at increasingly sophisticated levels between 400 and 500 times, and during each of those events has had a teacher at his side, if need be, to help him better manipulate.

A young adult who has "done his thing" before a group of his peers 250 times or more and who has gained a degree of poise before a group that he would not otherwise have had.

A young adult who can more easily look back and be conscious of relevance in his education, because there *has* been added significance to his study of literature, vocabulary, and grammar.

In short, a young adult who is quite possibly something more than a knowledgeable mute whose ideas of self-expression as often as not take the form of placards and obscenities.

SUMMARY

1. An effective composition program requires as much emphasis on the oral phase as the written phase. It is and has been obviously neglected in education to at least as great a degree as written composition.

2. Organization, creativeness, and perseverance are the keys to a successful oral composition program in your classroom.

3. Frequent oral presentations can be possible with the staggered schedule plan, which allows you to set aside specific and regular days for oral composition.

4. Book reports need not be more than a minute or so in length. And summary is not the only possibility for the report.

5. As with your writing program—perhaps to an even greater extent—oral composition must be student oriented. A student-led discussion should be considered the "exclusive" property of your students, with your intervention as part of the picture only when in your judgment it is absolutely necessary.

6. A round-robin resource unit is one workable plan for oral presentations over a year's time. The time you give your students to prepare material for these oral reports may vary all the way from 20 minutes to two weeks.

7. Some kind of evaluating tool should be used that establishes a private liaison between you and the student you are evaluating. It should point out strengths and weaknesses in the student's report and at least imply the ways in which the latter may be corrected.

8. To pursue the oral phase of active communicating with any less doggedness than your writing phase is to view it as less important—which it is not.

4

Balancing Your Course
with a Sensible Approach
to Grammar

 Virtually every student who enters my room in the fall—
and I'll wager, yours too—comes with the ability to coordinate
and subordinate clauses, in writing. He consistently places subjects before verbs except in instances of transposition. All of his
objects and complements fall generally in the "after" positions
of language structures. He uses an action verb when he wants
to express action; a non-action verb when he doesn't. His adjectives precede the nominals they modify when they are supposed
to; they follow the copulative in the predicate position when a
complement is called for. His adverbs are as ambulatory as
yours and mine. He generally positions modifying groups reasonably well relative to the words they modify. The great bulk
of his comparatives and superlatives are used correctly. He re-
sorts to the use of verbals with reckless abandon. And I must
further confess—though many of my colleagues claim I am putting them on—that without exception he does know how to
compose a sentence.

It seems oddly ritualistic, then, for you and I to have to intone in the language of syntax, week after week, just what it is he is doing when he writes a sentence. The process borders on the cabalistic when he is supplied with mysterious labels which when laid across the top of a sentence give it the appearance of an elaborate cryptogram. Which is what it may as well be for all the value it has in helping him learn how to use a language he has been using adequately for eleven or twelve years. The whole thing becomes grotesque when he is told to recall all these things in test form. Whether his score is high or low, several alternative conclusions *may* be assumed: (1) Some of his earlier teachers did their jobs well or badly; (2) His present teacher is doing his job well or badly; (3) He has an affinity for, or loathes analysis; (4) He memorizes readily or poorly; (5) He reacts to tests with confidence or trepidation. At least two things may not be assumed—that he is either good or bad at language manipulation.

Thirteen years of teaching English has led me to believe that the correlation (if one exists) between the teaching of grammar skills and the acquisition of communications skills is spectacularly insignificant, and the only time the former has any relevance to the latter is when one is communicating meaningfully. Good grammarians are not necessarily good writers. Neither are they necessarily bad. They are often mediocre. Bad grammarians are not necessarily bad writers. Neither are they necessarily good. They are often mediocre. But good, bad, or mediocre, your students, I believe, can more easily apply the principles of grammar while they are engaging in meaningful creative composition by simply compressing them into one solid proposition: How can I best make my writing clear and concise?

Techniques

That is why I think you will do well to lay major stress on teaching oral and written communications and minor stress on teaching grammar in your classroom. Have you ever considered teaching grammar doing no written drill, and reducing the

time spent on it to a small part of just one day a week? Why
not study syntax in the milieu of paragraphs—paragraphs
selected from your students' writing? That way you never
confront a sentence out of context, the kind you *always* confront in a conventional grammar text. With such a program
you would be giving grammar minor stress—in terms of time,
a maximum of ten hours a school year. That amounts to fifteen
minutes a week—minimal, to be sure, but in that time you can
manage to "grammarize" from a dozen to fifteen student paragraphs. By following a prescribed outline (which you will see
shortly) and studying syntax from some of their own compositions, most of your students will become aware of and be able
to identify English kernels and sentence patterns; come to recognize the two kinds of action and two kinds of non-action verbs
and their relationships to the patterns; become familiar with the
infinitive phrase and verb parts and know when participles are
verbals and when they are not; learn the principle of tense formation through combination; identify nominal functions and
be able to discuss whatever relationships they have to sentence
patterns; learn to see adjectives as "pre-noun" modifiers, adjective phrases as "post-noun" modifiers, and adverbs and adverb
phrases as "scatter" modifiers. This much exposure (theoretically, at least) will send them on to the next grade with the
grammar knowledge their teachers expect them to have learned,
which, alas, seems to be the only reason for the exposure at all.

The Grammar Text

Some English teachers—it seems to me—have been enslaved
by textbooks, specifically the grammar text. It should be evident
to us (if to any educators) that the average textbook's page after
page of language drill, with exercises comprised of totally unrelated ideas called sentences or terminal strings or whatever,
makes for a thoroughly stultifying experience for most students,
but apparently it is not evident. We *will* have our grammar
textbooks. Students at the secondary level of education, I sub-
mit, are no longer interested in the sentence, per se, particu-

larly if it is in a grammar text. They are concerned with *sentences,* preferably their own, which taken together relate to one another in developing one central theme. Furthermore, they are cognizant of the fact that in any given year they have never really been on the receiving end (except in rare cases) of an instructional program which allows them frequently and consistently to put their own sentences together in meaningful composition. The reality, of course, does not present itself to them in just those terms. Rather, they simply sense something is wrong and the feeling is manifested with variations on the theme, "Why do we have to learn all this grammar junk? We're never gonna use it." And their premise, I believe, is strikingly valid. In essence they are saying, "It is high time we stopped theorizing about what a sentence should look like and did something significant and creative with our language." *They want to communicate.* I am more and more convinced of this every year I teach. I am equally convinced that formal grammar teaching—except while students are creating with their language—is unwarranted in an English classroom beyond 5th grade, if indeed for that long. A better surmise perhaps would be that it should be taught from the beginning, but always in the context of creative expression.

Now, you and I would be the last to deny that the state of grammar teaching methodology is a fluid one. Today it is changing with a rapidity and regularity that was unknown in the past. Economically speaking, then, many grammar textbooks—even though they may contain composition programs as well—are a poor investment. Moreover, they tend to create and compound confusion with their constantly changing approaches and terminology. Besides, it seems to me, any English teacher can develop a far more imaginative and provocative writing program than is found in most texts.

A Substitute for the Grammar Text

But then there is that curriculum guide to contend with. We must teach grammar. And we must teach it as a separate entity with all of its prestigious and constantly changing terminology. Since there is no escaping it, why not do everything possible to lessen its traumatic effects? For instance, taken in its entirety, any grammar text can be compressed into a relatively innocuous three- or four-page outline. What's more, there is no valid reason why the sentences contained therein cannot enjoy a working relationship.

But before presenting your students with such an outline, it might be good practice to go into the history of English just briefly—or in some detail if you choose. In this regard, a large chart showing the Indo-European family with the Germanic branch more emboldened, is an excellent help. It should enjoy a prominent place in the front of your room—a convenient reference tool and visual aid the year round.

Having spent whatever length of time on history you deem adequate, it is a natural next step to say something to your students about the English language's relatively minor dependence on grammatical inflection, explaining that it utilizes word position instead—particularly with respect to nominals, verbs, and modifiers—as the significant factor in determining their functions in the sentence. These things said, I suppose it is well-nigh impossible to postpone the day of reckoning any longer. You have reached that point in time when you must begin teaching syntax in earnest.

The following represents the kind of outline which combined with student compositions can very ably substitute for any grammar text, seventh through twelfth grade, you might now be using. As you will see, it is a cursory treatment of the elements of grammar, but I believe an adequate one which forms a base for as thorough an exploration of syntax as you need to pursue:

Page 1

I—THE VERB. The sentence core.
   A—Action verb:
      1. Transitive verb—occurs in the S V DO or S V IO DO pattern:
        Jim sang a *song* to Claudia.
        He sang her a sentimental *melody.*

2. Intransitive verb—occurs in the S V_i pattern:
He sang with a style all his own.

B—Non-action verb:

1. Linking verb—occurs in the S V C pattern:
His *style was unique.* (Modification)
It was a soft *style.* (Co-identity)
2. Non-linking verb—occurs in the S V_{ni} pattern:
Claudia was under Jim's spell.

II—VERB PARTS

	to go (strong)	to play (weak)
A—Present	go	play
B—Past	went	played
C—Present participle	going	playing
D—Past participle	gone	played

E—Every verb consists of these four parts.

III—VERBALS

A—The infinitive—that phrase from which theoretically all verb forms derive. Always a verbal: The fans had come *to see* Starr at his best.

B—The past participle—a verbal only when it has no auxiliary:
Known for his expertise, the Packer quarterback was expected to produce.

C—The present participle—a verbal only when it has no auxiliary:
However, on this day, *producing* would be a little more difficult than usual.

IV—VERB TENSES

A—Present tense: The present and present participle parts form all variants of this tense.

B—Past tense: The past and past participle parts form all variants of this tense.

C—Variations of tense are arrived at through combination with modals, auxiliaries, and verbals.

Page 2

V—NOMINAL FUNCTIONS

A—Subject:
Starr crouched behind the center.

B—Direct object:
Detroit shifted its *linebackers.*

C—Indirect object:
The center gave *Starr* the football.

D—Object of the preposition:
Starr clutched the ball and faded back into the *pocket*.

E—Subject complement:
Now it was his *show*.

F—Noun in apposition:
Suddenly two huge hulks, Detroit *linebackers,* descended on Starr and crushed him to the turf.

G—Subject and object of the verbal:
Bart quietly asked the *referee* to peel *him* off the gridiron.

H—Possessive noun:
As he returned to the huddle, the spunky *quarterback's* face showed grim determination.

Page 3

VI—MODIFIERS

A—Adjective—modifier of the nominal.
1. Most often immediately precedes the noun it modifies:
The *determined* Packers lined up again.
2. However, the adjective frequently modifies the subject from the predicate side of the sentence:
Starr was the most *determined* of all.

B—Adverb—modifies anything but nominals.
1. Can be found in virtually any position in the sentence and is often far removed from the word it modifies:
Once again he barked signals *loudly*.
Carefully he manipulated the long, staccato count.
The center *again* snapped the ball, this time *more crisply*.

C—Degrees of adjectives and adverbs:

Positive	Comparative	Superlative
good	better	best
lovely	lovelier	loveliest
beautiful	more beautiful	most beautiful
fast	faster	fastest
rapidly	more rapidly	most rapidly

D—The group modifier
1. The adjective-phrase modifier is almost always found immediately following the noun it modifies: Starr, without a trace *of hesitation,* moved back.
2. The position of the adverb-phrase modifier, like that of the adverb, is not nearly so stable as that of the adjective-phrase modifier: *With supreme finesse* he raised his hand *as if to pass,* and then slanted *off tackle, through the secondary,* and on *to pay-dirt.*

The above outline, you will notice, carries through the phrase modifier which I think is as far as one need progress in the junior high school grades. For grades 10 through 12, then, part "D" of section "VI" would contain four parts, points 3 and 4 covering adjective and adverb clause modifiers, respectively. For the nominal clause an additional section "VII" would be in order:

3. As with the adjective-phrase modifier, the adjective-clause modifier most commonly follows the noun it modifies: The crowd, *which numbered 50,000-plus,* stood up as one, their cheers rending the crisp fall air.
4. And as with the adverb and adverb-phrase modifier, instability marks the adverb-clause modifier's position with respect to the word it modifies: *As the Packers lined up for the conversion,* four young fans strode along the sidelines carrying a gigantic sign reading STARR FOR PRESIDENT.

VII—THE NOMINAL CLAUSE
A—As subject:
1. *That he could be elected to the nation's highest office* was doubted by no one in the stands.

And so forth with the direct object, indirect object, complement, object of the preposition, and object of the verbal clauses.

Now, if you happen to be using the transformational generative approach in your school system, you will perhaps (though not necessarily) have to increase the number of basic patterns, but the above outline system will still do nicely. In transformational symbols, the S V DO pattern becomes two distinct patterns

—NP + VT, and NP + v-have + NP, or possibly just the former. The S V_i pattern is expressed as NP + VI + adv. The S V C pattern is NP + v-be + adj or NP, and NP + VL + adj or NP, or again, possibly just the former. And the S V_{nl} pattern becomes NP + v-be + adv. Incidentally, the transformational generative approach to grammar seems to be the best argument going for taking grammar out of the English classroom and making it an elective. Its mathematical, highly detailed, complex (but not always consistent), and often ponderous nature simply preclude any teacher's doing justice to it (if indeed it deserves justice) in addition to all the other facets of English curriculum during a given academic year.

How is the outline better than a text? I don't know for sure that it is, *but it does have the advantage of consolidation and sentence-relatedness which most texts do not have.* Taken a page at a time, each elaborated upon in the context of student writing, I think it can be just as effective as the conventional grammar text, if not more so.

Before its implementation in conjunction with your students' writing takes place, it is advisable, I think, to take your classes through page one of the outline on a discussion basis to familiarize them with whatever approach to the teaching of syntax you are using. When you have gone through this initial instructional phase carefully, your students are better able to apply the principles propounded in the outline to actual language units. They are ready for what is in effect the first phase of their study of syntax.

Analysis of Syntax Within Student Writing

To be specific, you begin with kernels, patterns, the verb, and related material, as delineated on page one of the outline. This takes anywhere from three to six 15-minute sessions. Following that, give each of your students a page of three or four dittoed paragraphs selected from their own writing, and simply proceed with the business at hand; that is, identifying kernels, patterns, verbs, verbals, and the combinations which produce tense. The process is implemented solely through class discussion. If students wish to write in identifying labels, they may do so. You may even want to make the practice mandatory, although I can't imagine why. At fifteen minutes a week, it takes about nine weeks to labor through a page of paragraphs. At its conclusion, presentation of page two of the outline takes place, following the same procedure as with page one, and another page of student paragraphs is circulated. Now the process becomes cumulative: you carry out your language analysis in terms of pages one *and* two of the outline. And so it goes through the third and last page of the outline.

For demonstration purposes let's work a bit with a student paragraph, "UFO's," by Dave Zentner, and assume we have reached the third quarter of our study of syntax:

A bright light streaks across the darkened sky, reddish in comparison with the white stars twinkling behind it. Suddenly, dipping down from its path through the heavens, it begins to chase an automobile cruising along a lonely highway. The driver, trying to avoid this huge red ball of intense light following him, misjudges a curve and his car rolls over into a ditch and he goes into a permanent sleep. What was that red light? The air force calls it a UFO. Where did it come from? We may never know.

Sentence one. Kernel: *Light streaks.* Pattern: $S \ V_i$. Nominal functions: *sky, comparison, stars, it*—all objects of prepositions. Single-word modifiers: *bright,* modifying light; *darkened,* modifying sky; *reddish,* modifying light. Phrase modifiers: *across the darkened sky,* modifying streaks; *in comparison,* modifying reddish; *with the white stars,* modifying comparison; *behind it,* modifying twinkling. And so on. From an instructional standpoint you might remind students as you go along that: (1) the number of words in the kernel equals the number of symbols in its pattern, (2) all of the objects occur in what could be called an "after" position, (3) the single-word modifiers are all adjectives and with the exception of "reddish," all of them immediately precede the nouns they modify, (4) only one of the phrase-modifiers is adjectival, following immediately the noun it modifies, and that the other phrases are reasonably "unscattered" considering they are all adverb phrases. You might also want to comment on the natty bit of imbedding manifested in the paragraph.

As you can see, we "grammarized" cumulatively, using the instructional material from all three of the outline pages. Early in the year, there would be simply kernel and pattern identification with verb recognition in terms of transitive, intransitive, linking, and non-linking, plus ferreting out verbals—all concepts delineated on page one of the outline.

Can you see that analyzing language in the setting of paragraphs like this is far more attractive than in a grammar text with its truncated, uninteresting language? I think it is evident from the above paragraph just how mature some students have become in language manipulation. I'm thinking in particular of the adjective and verbal clusters used so effectively in Dave's paragraph. To use this kind of language unit for the study of syntax would seem logical and practical, but to subject the caliber of student who wrote it to massive textbook sentence drill would be, in my estimation, nothing short of sadistic.

Let me point out that this whole process is not exactly going to titillate your students. Hardly any of them are going to get choked up over a cool S V C or S V DO pattern, and seldom will there be cries of "I found it! I found it!" when they are hunting for a verbal or a modifier or whatever. The subject matter of grammar is just not conducive to ecstasy for most adolescents. Nothing bears this fact out quite as lucidly as the year-end course evaluations my students write for me: "I don't think there is anything that can be done with it, it's just a rotten subject." "I feel that grammar is a complete waste of time. No offense." "It is kind of boring and I guess you need to know it but I doubt it." However, I assure you, it is far less irritating than the conventional textbook approach which I found antagonized students to a point just short of violent demonstrations. And it must be remembered that though grammar study continues throughout the year, it is in this kind of program for only 15 minutes at a time and just once a week—the "short burst" method. You have done away, then, with tedious sentence drill *in* as well as *out* of class, and your having to occupy yourself with the trivia of correcting drillwork, the value of which in terms of student enlightenment, was highly questionable to begin with.

Testing

There is no reason why you have to test your students on this material any more than three specific times; that is, at the completion of each page of paragraphs. You may be able to give a fourth test—if time allows—at the end of the year, but there would seem to be nothing to gain by doing so, except another 150 papers to correct. Perhaps you won't feel it necessary to test them at all. But if you do, I recommend you use only multiple-choice statements which follow the outline pages exactly. Design your tests in such a way that they reflect the instructional program itself; that is, so that the material they cover is cumulative. As has been said earlier, this kind of test requires a very short time to correct—a class of 30 to 35 papers, ten minutes. To make the exam as much a learning as a testing experience, why don't you try the programed learning method, or perhaps one that resembles it? For example, test number one might be as follows:

1. The two principal divisions of the verb are action and (a) transitive (b) non-action (c) linking.
2. Action and non-action are the two main categories of the (a) noun (b) transitive verb (c) verb.
3. There are two kinds of action verb, (a) transitive and intransitive (b) non-linking and transitive (c) linking and non-linking.
4. Transitive is one kind of action verb, the other is (a) linking (b) intransitive (c) non-linking.
5. A transitive verb is completed by a direct object. An intransitive verb is (a) completed (b) preceded (c) not completed by a direct object.
6. The S V DO pattern always contains (a) a linking verb (b) a transitive verb (c) an intransitive verb.
7. The S V_i pattern always contains (a) a linking verb (b) a transitive verb (c) an intransitive verb.

8. Transitive and intransitive verbs have one thing in common. They are both (a) non-action verbs (b) linking verbs (c) action verbs.
9. There are two kinds of non-action verbs, linking and (a) action (b) intransitive (c) non-linking.
10. Non-linking is one kind of non-action verb; the other is (a) action (b) intransitive (c) linking.
11. The S V C pattern contains a (a) transitive verb (b) linking verb (c) non-linking verb.
12. The complement is linked to the subject by a (a) non-linking verb (b) linking verb (c) transitive verb.
13. The kind of non-action verb found in an S V_{nl} pattern is (a) linking (b) non-linking (c) transitive.
14. Linking and non-linking verbs have one thing in common. They are both (a) non-action verbs (b) action verbs (c) transitive verbs.
15. Every verb consists of (a) two parts (b) five parts (c) four parts.
16. In any sentence, two of those parts, the present participle and past participle, to be verbs, always require (a) a helper (b) an ending (c) a preposition.
17. If the participles are not accompanied by a helper, they are always (a) verbs (b) verbals (c) last.
18. In any sentence the other two verb parts are always (a) verbs (b) verbals (c) participles, whether they are accompanied by helpers or not.
19. The other kind of verbal is always a phrase called an (a) infinitive (b) auxiliary (c) adverb.
20. In any sentence, the infinitive is always a phrase and always a (a) verbal (b) verb (c) participle.
21. There are only (a) two (b) three (c) six basic tenses in the English language.
22. Present and past are the two basic (a) verbs (b) tenses (c) helpers in English.
23. Variations of tense are arrived at through (a) combination (b) elimination (c) transformation.
24. Combination of verb parts with modals and helpers produces various shades of (a) verb (b) verbal (c) tense.

Ridiculously simple as tests go? Well, simple at any rate. But more importantly, I think it teaches as it moves along. If a student is thinking at all, and is interested (a questionable premise, I suppose), he can come out of a test like this more knowledgeable than when he went in. Even if I thought the present approaches to grammar teaching had anything going for them, I'd still give tests like this one.

It might interest you to know that the scored results of these tests, when related individually to student writing ability, invariably suggest the continued elusiveness of that much-sought-after correlation referred to earlier—if you want to take the trouble to look for it. Continued grammar testing is hardly of any use in the accumulation of comparative data, since I no longer grade student compositions, but the last year I did, the results revealed nothing new regarding correlation between the two. You may judge for yourself. In any event, the following raw data I think will interest you:

85 students were involved and all were given three grammar tests. The grades of oral and written compositions numbered from a low of 52 to as many as 66 per student and were averaged four weeks into the fourth quarter. "Poor" rating was E to F; "average," D to C; and "good," B to A. The results were as follows:

	Grammar	Composition
Poor	27	0
Average	29	43
Good	29	42

More than anything these figures reveal (1) the teacher's lack of enthusiasm for grammar teaching, and (2) his high grading habits with regard to student composition. They certainly suggest no significant relationship between grammar learning and ability to write. For example, eight of the "poor" grammarians, nearly half the "average" grammarians, and slightly over half the "good" grammarians ended up in the "good" category on the composition side. The rest were average writers.

But if you'd like something of a more conclusive nature with respect to this matter, let me quote from my article in *Today's Education* for December of 1968:

According to a 1963–64 experiment with matched groups of students in grades 10–12 at Ross Sheppard High School in Edmonton, Alberta, Canada, "The findings of this study support those of earlier studies that knowledge of traditional grammar is but poorly related to ability to write and that this same poor relationship is apparently found when more recent grammatical theories are used, in this case, transformational theory. The actual practical value of teaching any kind of grammar is still very much in doubt, even though this value seems to be almost the only one ever cited for such teaching . . . ." [1]

Student Writing Reflects Few Problems with Grammar

But to get back to more important things, the preponderance of problems in student writing are not grammatical at all; they are overwhelmingly in the areas of spelling, punctuation, and alas, imaginativeness—or rather, the lack of it. But then, whatever the problem, it is hardly going to be discovered at any time other than when your students are manipulating the language in meaningful, and it is hoped, creative composition under your supervision. It is here, it seems to me, and only here, that grammar should be taught, and whenever possible in anything but syntactical terms. Is grammar terminology of any significance, for instance, to the writing student who doesn't know an adjective phrase from an adverb phrase? And is he necessarily more likely to place one or the other badly in a sentence than the student who does know the difference? When a student combines an infinitive phrase with a verb or uses one as a nominal, why must he know its name? Must he who has just composed an S V DO sentence pattern know that he is in the presence of a transitive verb? Why must students know that adjectives are pre-noun modifiers when they always put them in that position anyway? How practical is it to call the sense verbs (seem, appear, taste, feel, smell, et cetera) linking verbs when students constantly use them not only as action verbs, but in the non-linking sense as well? Et cetera, et cetera.

---

[1] "Grammar Should Be Groovier," *Today's Education,* December 1968, page 62.

Why This Kind of Program?

The kind of program we have been discussing is designed as much for the convenience of the teacher as the student. Certainly it has its weaknesses, but I think it can be illustrated rather conclusively that the textbook-written-drillwork approach has far more, the most significant of which is its profligate waste of student and teacher time and energy which could better be spent in more fruitful activities. I believe it can be further illustrated that finding names for, and labeling all of the elements of one's language, and then examining students on their ability to remember what the names and labels are, borders on the trifling. It is a classic example of "student-stuffing" referred to earlier. Syntax, taught in isolation but as part of the English classroom experience, as is now the case, would make far more sense if it were completely isolated, made an elective, and placed in another classroom.

A Re-evaluation

The grammar syndrome seems to be a product of the curriculum guide to the same degree that the anti-communications-skills syndrome is. Added to the problem is the nature of the subject matter of grammar versus that of composition. On the one hand the teacher is confronted with explicit sets of instructions on specific page numbers of a specific text to be completed over specific periods of time. On the other hand, by comparison, the writing program (if one is delineated) is a nebulous thing at best, and this is what most debilitates the teacher. Such a condition need not be; it is simply a matter of re-establishing our values and setting new priorities: Which is more important, the teaching of grammar skills or the teaching of communications skills? We should blush at even having to ask the question.

SUMMARY

1. The intuitive grammar of your students, that is, their built-in system of syntax, acquired through years

of using the language, makes prolonged exposure to grammar study isolated from composition completely senseless.

2. The most effective vehicle for students to gain a knowledge of good usage is written composition under your careful supervision.

3. Fifteen minutes of grammar study a week from a three- or four-page outline, the principles of which are put to use while studying syntax from their own writing, is sufficient for your students.

4. Testing may be eliminated entirely or limited to three distinct tests, the first covering page one of the outline, the latter two covering the outline material cumulatively. Use of the programed learning technique on your tests seems feasible and can make your tests learning as well as measuring devices.

5. Any attempt at establishing a correlation between grammar study and ability in written composition among students seems a waste of time.

6. This kind of grammar program is an advantage to both teacher and student, but a still more realistic approach to the matter would seem to be the removal of grammar study entirely from the English classroom and making it an elective.

5

Alternatives in the Teaching
of Vocabulary

It continues to mystify me as to why in most school systems, vocabulary (mistakenly referred to as spelling) is offered through the eighth grade—sometimes longer—in a form with multiple inherent weaknesses, namely, the vocabulary workbook. Granted, the workbook is usually elaborately and painstakingly designed to help students anatomize words, using a variety of approaches, and granted further that it is well thought out and if used properly by the student, just has to help him build onto his vocabulary.

The trouble is that too many students do not use it advantageously. They frequently ignore the workbook's sequential structure, beginning the exercises anywhere but at the beginning, and occasionally even resort to mere blank-filling, which artifice is supposed to leave their teachers with the impression that the assignment is completed. (It sometimes works, doesn't it?) Another of its weaknesses is the possibility of the drill in the workbook becoming an end in itself. I can cite any number of cases in my experience, of students who just never get around to the "nitty-gritty" of spelling and meaning because they become preoccupied with the written part of the workbook lesson. Hence, more often than not they score badly in the test, although their workbook is complete and relatively accurate. Perhaps the most patently weak point of the vocabulary workbook, however, is the maximum opportunity it presents for inter-student collaboration—tending to approach at times the proportions of an orgy among some students—the settings for which are places like the lunchroom, rest room, homeroom, library, and both ends of the telephone.

You are familiar with these drawbacks, all of which are viewed more or less as phenomena about which nothing much can be done. And indeed as long as the workbook is an integral part of the instructional edifice of word-learning, such weaknesses will not only remain, but I fear, become magnified in terms of the damage they can do to English students.

If the system in which you teach requires the use of a workbook, I should like to suggest that it has outlived its usefulness. It is hardly doing the job it was intended to do, simply because you cannot allow it to. Its architects seem to have designed it as if vocabulary were the only thing being taught in the language classroom, for to be ideally effective, all of its exercises would have to be done within the classroom environment under your supervision, and such a practice would require at least three, if not four or five full periods a week. To utilize this kind of study aid under any other conditions, I believe, is unrealistic. In short, I think it is fair to say that a workbook in the teaching of language is just too ponderous and impractical an instrument to be used under laboratory conditions, which is really the only effective way it can be used.

Having said this, I can see no reason why the same approach to vocabulary teaching that is used at the senior high school level cannot be used at the junior high level as well; namely, effecting student exposure to words through dictionary use, the literature they read, and periodic circulation of lists of significant words compiled by the teacher. The programed learning approach, though relatively new, seems promising. Lyons & Carnahan's *Programed Vocabulary* treats vocabulary learning in a most interesting manner. The text is a workbook, but one which can be used readily under laboratory conditions, since it is far less ponderous than the conventional vocabulary workbook. Developed by James I. Brown, Professor of Rhetoric at the University of Minnesota, *Programed Vocabulary* utilizes the principle of mnemonics—a method for improving the memory—in which students are able to make a series of associations relative to each word they study, every association in effect reinforcing the infor- ⟋ mation derived from the previous associations. Dr. Brown uses 14 English words as his base of study—that is, what he refers to as the 14 most important roots which also contain the 20 most important prefixes. Besides being ideal for learning vocabulary under laboratory conditions, the programed learning technique allows each student to move along at his own pace and at least theoretically reduces the necessity for a weekly test.

Emphasize Word-Meaning

Vocabulary curriculum has one other inherent weakness which has nothing to do with workbooks, however. It is the overemphasis on spelling, at least implying that word-meaning and pronunciation are of secondary importance. I think first of all that we English teachers at every grade level should stop using the term "spelling" in reference to this part of the curriculum. This may seem like nit-picking to you, but it really is a matter of accurate communication. If you tell a student he is to do his spelling over the week, or for tomorrow, that is usually exactly what he is going to do. He is going to learn how to spell the words in the lesson you assign, and more than likely that is all he is going to do. "Vocabulary study" or "word anatomy" or some such title as that suggests a much more inclusive approach. Even then you have got to spell it out for him in terms of which words he is likely to be unfamiliar with and therefore must go to the dictionary for a more thorough understanding of. Second, there has to be an in-depth probe of word-meaning (written and/or oral) with the study of each lesson, at which time proper pronunciation is certain to be brought out. And third, I think it is incumbent upon us to convince students of the uselessness of a word whose meaning they do not know. All of this unfortunately has to be done in the classroom for the most part on a given day of each week—weeks which are already overburdened with curriculum—and on that one day you just have to cover a lot of ground.

Techniques

If in your school system the vocabulary workbook is mandatory, I fervently hope you don't check each workbook lesson at deskside (or otherwise) every week as I used to. The workbook's drawbacks pointed out earlier would seem to make such a practice patently trivial and apparently ineffective: One assumes that the "threat" of having his homework checked regularly increases the probability that a student will complete it. You have probably discovered as I have that the assumption is hardly valid. In the days when I was still checking individual workbooks, nearly 50 per cent of my students did assignments either partially or not at all. And yet, of that approximately 50 per cent, well over half carried "A" and "B" test averages in the course.

Instead of checking individual workbooks each week, why not give the written work in the book optional status, concentrating on dictionary work, allowing students to complete the exercises if they wish to, and stipulating that if they complete all of the material accurately and legibly, it will be given extra credit status?

If you make the workbook optional—and I believe the reasons for doing so are valid—then I think it follows that you would be better off without a workbook at all, since under these conditions it turns out to be nothing more nor less than an appurtenance which just happens to have in it a year's supply of words to be learned. A pocket dictionary serves the same end and carries an added advantage of much more detailed information about each word, especially as to meaning. Students need a great deal more experience with the dictionary, anyway, and the workbook approach makes it too easy for them to neglect word-meaning—unless, of course, its exercises are completed under what we referred to above as "laboratory conditions." Further exposure to vocabulary learning can and must come through your literature and composition teaching. Indeed, the vocabulary learning which takes place through these two media is equal in importance to, if not more important, than that which takes place in isolated study. Any discussion which follows a reading lesson can be at least partially oriented toward vocabulary study. Hence, in a group reading situation, one of the activities each week in connection with whatever material is being read, would certainly be the compilation by all of your students of the troublesome words they come across in their reading. On discussion day, then, at least part of the period would be spent in vocabulary exploration.

Students, I think you will agree, learn and remember words and their proper uses more readily in the context of meaningful literature than in the isolation of itemization. Furthermore, it is often possible for them to arrive at the correct meaning of a word merely by looking carefully at the other elements with it in the sentence or paragraph environment. With respect to composition, the learning of vocabulary is especially significant. When a student is conscientiously engaged in creative expression, he is constantly searching for that better word. If he has a dictionary at his desk (I use "if" advisedly) he may or may not find it, but the chances of enhancing his vocabulary are at least increased simply because he is working with a dictionary. And in your deskside visits during writing sessions, suggesting more precise nouns or vigorous verbs or effective modifiers to students has a way of subtly emphasizing the importance of vocabulary learning that workbook and literature-oriented vocabulary study do not have. At the senior high school level, the use of composition as a vehicle for vocabulary learning is of particular importance since at this level vocabulary study, per se, has nowhere near the position of importance (not that it is less so) in language curriculum that it does in the first eight grades.

Testing

Of course, weekly tests are a part of the vocabulary phase of your program, and I'm sure you are aware that the options on type are extremely limited—to two, as a matter of fact. You can administer the written spelling-meaning type or the spelling-only type. Have you tried using both kinds alternately for any length of time? The technique works very well. It can certainly add variety to your program. The former consists of 33 words (or whatever number you are administering), six to ten of which are specified as words to be used correctly in sentences—one word to a sentence. You may, if you wish, exercise another option here, that of giving your students an opportunity to incorporate the designated words into a paragraph or more, with the stipulation that if the resulting composition is reasonably well done, it will be worth an "A" grade (forgive me) in addition to the grade received on the spelling part of the test. If it is done poorly, they lose nothing for having tried, provided they have used the test words correctly in the sentences of their composition. They get "A" on the composition or no grade at all on it. The idea obviously is to encourage students to pursue still more in the way of creative expression—with that ubiquitous grade as bait—at the same time adding still more variety to your vocabulary program.

Initially, you will perhaps be disappointed in the small numbers of students who are adventuresome enough to go for the option. Stick with it, though, and occasionally strengthen incentive with a short pep talk, pointing up the fact that they really have nothing to lose by trying it. Enthusiasm, I assure you, will increase and added numbers will exercise the option the longer you continue the practice.

I hasten to add (once again) you will get some remarkably good material as a result. Some of your students will occasionally even attempt a poem—which takes some doing under circumstances such as these. Not long ago, one unusually creative young lady in a morning class of mine did so with marked suc-

cess. On the particular day in question, I had my class check ten
of the test words to be used in sentences *or* a composition. Here
is what our young poet came up with. The test words are italicized in the text of the poem:

> The *brilliant* sun shone over the meadows
>> while the *selfish* buttercups tried to hog it.
>>> By some *oversight* God made the tulips taller.
>
> While *elaborate* roses with red petals
>> intricately spaced and placed on yellow heads
>>> —*noble* in their *appearance* and stance—
>>>> took *inventory* of the others when the wind blew,
>>>>> *ambitious* violets strained to reach the sun,
>>>>>> but unable to *maintain* themselves, fell.

Democracy does not flourish in gardens.[1]

Moving up and down the rows, I just happened to stop at the
young lady's desk as she sat composing. I don't mind telling you
I was impressed. I remained there as unobtrusively as possible
until she reached "democracy," where she was obviously
stumped. Together we came up with that last line. Which line,
and more specifically, "gardens," perhaps is inappropriate inasmuch as the scene opens in the meadows. That seems unimportant, however, when one studies the composition as a whole. Besides, I think it is evident that the poem, for all that, could have
ended at the word "fell" in the previous line.

You will come across some good prose too. Here are three
fairly representative examples, the first, a piece of facetious narrative, the second and third, very readable commentaries. Again,
the words chosen from the test are italicized for these particular
enterprises, just six in number. First, the narrative:

Gluepot

Gluepot was *altogether* an absolute wreck. She was just a pile
of bones held together with a few sinewy muscles, if you could call
them muscles. A *bridle* could no longer be shoved in her mouth

---

[1] Valerie Williams is the authoress.

because she had no teeth to hold it in place. Her *elaborate* silver
show equipment studded with jewels was tarnished black from dis-
use. The *judgment* passed on poor Gluepot was that she be made
into glue. The *management* had made that decision two weeks ago
and now the truck was here. Their one *oversight* was that Virginia,
the boss's daughter, loved that bag of bones deeply. She was heart-
broken. Most stories have a happy ending. This one doesn't. In
fact, this one doesn't have any ending at all.[2]

And a commentary, a product of the same lesson:

A horse is *altogether* different from other animals. One difference
is that it can be ridden while most other animals cannot. Horses
need special equipment which can be quite expensive and *elaborate*. One of the most important pieces of equipment is the *bridle*.
A horse is not very hard to ride once you get used to it. Good
management is needed to show the horse who is boss. *Judgment*
is not as important as when driving a car, as the horse knows what
he can go through and what he can't. While a horse is not very
hard to ride, one *oversight* can lead to a very painful accident.[3]

Another commentary from another lesson:

When in the course of human events it becomes necessary for
one nation to *dissolve* the political bonds. . . . These are the first
words of the document used to declare our independence from England. Our nation has changed rapidly since then. We have come all
the way from a small weak nation to the great *institution* we are
today. Today we are one of the most powerful nations in the world.
We buy goods from other nations and to thank us for our *patronage*
they buy goods from us. Even though we are powerful today it does
not *necessarily* mean we will be a great nation in the future. It is
hard to *perceive* what we will be in the future. We have many problems today and if they get worse we will probably become what is
known as a "backward nation." We need *available* a machine that
tells what will happen in the future. Then maybe we could solve
our problems before they get worse.[4]

It is interesting to observe what words students choose for
their topic sentences. For instance, in the lesson which contained
the word "bridle," not more than two or three students chose it

---

[2] The author is Tom Stieghorst.
[3] Tom Glatch is the author.
[4] The author is Jeff Smidt.

as the key word in their topic sentence, but the vast majority struck on it as the key word with regard to the subject matter of their paragraphs.

I feel compelled to warn you that this kind of test can be discouraging to you, particularly with respect to students who not only decline to exercise the option, but who obviously use the designated words in sentences in a way which leads you to suspect they did not concentrate much, if any, on word-meaning in the current lesson. When week after week you read sentences like, "We have a very good *compliance*"; "I am *contemplating* to think about buying a bike"; "Americans *waist* a lot of food"; "He followed the same *trial* through the woods"; "The boy's *melancholy* was not happy"; et cetera, the temptation to abandon the technique will perhaps seem overwhelming. Yet if you take the trouble to determine just how many of your students are doing this kind of thing on their tests, I think you'll find the numbers to be relatively small. If, however, you find evidence to the contrary, then perhaps you will want to shift to the spelling-only type test which of course eliminates the necessity of your correcting any part of the vocabulary tests at all, since this technique adapts admirably to inter-student correcting. In the week that you give the word-spelling-meaning test (if you alternate the two types), you can still utilize inter-student correcting of the spelling part, but it is obviously necessary for you to collect the papers and correct the word-meaning part of the test yourself. Using the spelling-only kind of test, however, does create a strong possibility that word-meaning is going to be neglected unless you supplement the test with some kind of word-meaning exercise. And there is only one really practical way you can do this, I believe; preface each test with a discussion period, concentrating exclusively on the meaning and pronunciation of words which in one way or another might give students trouble. The discussion technique can continue, of course, as you administer the test.

On your vocabulary day, then, you can spend the first fifteen or twenty minutes of the period ferreting out student problems with the current lesson, especially pertinent to word-meaning.

Then, during the test you can stop at previously designated words with discussion and questioning. The italicized sentences are stage directions for you, the teacher:

"Acquaintance. Jill, can you use the word correctly in a sentence?" *Smile as if you were on Candid Camera.*

"My sister always does her homework correctly."

Your chance to exercise monumental restraint. Still smiling, you clarify things. "The word is 'acquaintance,' Jill. Can you use it in a sentence for us?"

(After an uncomfortably long silence and much grimacing.) "That girl is an acquaintance of mine."

"Good. Al, what does 'acquaintance' mean in that sentence?"

"Like when you know somebody?"

"I asked you first, Al." *Point finger of left hand straight up and cock head to right.*

"Like when you know somebody."

"Can you put that in better English?" *Pyramid hands studiously in front of face.*

"Like somebody you know."

(Not exactly the king's English, but progress nonetheless.) "Okay, Al." (*Unenthusiastically*)

That is, you ask individual students to use significant words correctly in sentences—those words which most of them obviously are not going to know the meaning or meanings of without consulting the dictionary. Use words which have a high mortality rate among adolescents: words with multiple meanings; words preceded or followed by peculiar structures; words that have multi-class functions; words with homonyms; et cetera. If a sentence is not specific enough to point out a word's meaning, then it is possible with the oral approach to question other students about its meaning and continue until someone uses it more definitively:

Or, following a slightly different tack:

"Democrat. Carol, which do you think is more precise, 'Henry Reuss is a member of the democrat party', or 'Henry Reuss is a member of the democratic party'?" *Stand up and fold arms, squinting eyes in obvious concentration.*

"Henry Reuss is a member of the democratic party."

"Why?"

"It sounds better."

"Carl?" *Open eyes wide as if you expect spectacular revelation.*

"Democrat party is more accurate, I think, because both parties do things the democratic way—or they say they do, anyway."

"Okay, Carl. Yes, Gail?"

"The dictionary doesn't say that 'democrat' is an adjective, though."

"Good point. What about that, Carl?" *Hand on chin.*

"There are lots of things the dictionary doesn't say."

"Then you think we can make words do what we want them to do, regardless of the dictionary?" *Arch eyebrows in anticipation.*

"Sure, why not?"

"Well, let me ask you this. Which came first, dictionaries or language?" *Effect the inscrutable gaze of an historian.*

"Language, because dictionaries wouldn't have anything in 'em if it wasn't for language."

"Very good, Carl. As a matter of fact, dictionaries are pretty recent additions in the study of language since written language is relatively recent. Couldn't we say, then, that one or the other of the two words does the job suitably? . . ." *Attempt nonchalance as if you expected all such word exploration to turn out this well.*

This kind of procedure has at least one advantage over the use of test sentences, that of flexibility. It is possible to do a great many more things with word-meaning orally, and therefore it enables you to approach it from many more angles. At the senior high school level, the discussion technique, through your students' reading assignments and issuance of weekly or quarterly lists of vocabulary builders upon which to base further class discussions, is entirely adequate. And, as pointed out before, if your writing program is a well-structured, weekly operation in your overall course, the matter of vocabulary learning there can become highly individualized through your suggestions with respect to a student's word choice in his composition. And it is wise, I think, to remember that students acquire considerable vocabulary on their own.

Words Can Be Fun

With all its problems, vocabulary study need never be dull. On your test day, you and your students can carry on a constant dialogue, ranging from banter to serious discussion, and it is only after you have finished dictating their lesson that the room need settle down into an exam atmosphere, at which time it is helpful to give the class two or three minutes to correct any penmanship and/or spelling errors on their papers. Of course, with the spelling-word-meaning test you will have to allow your students at least fifteen minutes beyond the spelling test itself, to compose their sentences or compositions.

Composing sentences out of thin air as you are dictating a vocabulary lesson seems to me to invite entertainment. A teacher can let his hair down then as at no other time. For one thing, it is one of the few times that he has undisputed possession of the floor if he wants it. For another, he is improvising—or can pretend to be—which always creates an atmosphere for discussion and very often "humor":

> "Olives. Mike, may olives be eaten with the fingers?"
> "Yes, I guess so."
> "Wrong, Mike, the fingers should be eaten separately." (*Moans.*)
> "Police. Karen, can you tell me what a police cookie is?"

"A cop cake." (*Years pass before you get the right answer to that one.*)

"Generally. Washington, Pershing, and Eisenhower were all outstanding men, generally speaking." (*Delayed action groans or no reaction at all.*)

"Blizzard. Mother cut open the chicken and pulled out its blizzard." (*Variety of sounds.*)

And, on the more serious side again:

"Fortune. 'Truth is no road to fortune.' Pete, can you tell us anything about the character of the man who wrote that? He lived in 18th century France."

"Was he a poor man?"

Frown as if confused. "Why poor, Pete?"

"Well, he sounds bitter."

"Why, I suppose he was bitter, judging by his statement. Does that necessarily mean he was poor?"

"No, I guess not, but it could be a clue."

"Sandy?" *Very quickly rising from your chair, startling the class to attention.*

"Maybe he was surrounded by hoods."

"How do you know he wasn't one himself?" *Victory grin.*

"I don't know—maybe he was."

"Does his statement perhaps suggest something about the times?"

"Not necessarily."

"Why do you say that, Sandy?" *Assume your most quizzical look.*

"Well, I've heard people nowadays say things like that."

"Good point." *Grin lavishly.* "Yes, Lisa?"

"Wasn't there a revolution there then?"

"When?"

"In the 18th century?"

"What does that have to do with 'Truth is no road to

fortune'?" *Pretending confidence that the discussion is moving toward a satisfactory conclusion.*

"I don't know, but there must have been a reason for the revolution."

"I wonder what it was. Yes, Gary?"

"Rotten government . . . poverty . . . hunger?"

"Very good, Gary. Can we relate this to our statement?"

"Corruption?"

"What about it, Gary?" *Pained look of expectancy.*

"Well, the guy is saying it doesn't pay to be honest, or something like that, and that's being corrupt, I guess . . ."

Nod head studiously, exhibiting grin of satisfaction.

There is in this kind of exchange the danger of suddenly discovering the period has nearly ended while you are still administering your test, and then there is only one thing to do; have your students exchange papers and correct their unfinished products. But experience makes the difference, and you learn to regulate these periods of involvement without thinking about it so that your students have at least ten minutes to correct and score one another's papers.

Inter-Student Correcting

Inter-student correcting of papers is a marvelous time-saver—as you well know—and an entirely valid technique, but constant hand-raising by students to question you regarding some technicality in the correcting process, such as to circle or not to circle an undotted "i" or an uncrossed "t" can be self-defeating. The only solution I can think of to the problem is that you absolutely disallow it. Yes, it works. If you make it amply clear to your students that *they* are correcting the test and that any decision they make is theirs alone to make without the need to consult you, they will do it that way. Occasionally a student will insist on raising his hand to question you, but you need only remind him that *he* is correcting the test. You might add that if he should make a wrong decision, the world will still likely continue its counterclockwise rotation on the morrow. Whether or not you consider undotted i's or uncrossed t's errors is something you have to make known to them at the outset, however.

Drillwork

Is drilling of misspelled words effective? As with so many other questions in education, this one is just about unanswerable. Perhaps we should ask, "Is it necessary?" This one I think could be more easily answered, and I would be tempted to say no. I would guess that both questions could be answered in the negative. If you make your students report to you within a day or two after their test and orally spell the words they missed, you are, in my judgment, pursuing a wiser course. If, however, you require written word drill, you would do well to keep it at ten times or under for each misspelled word. Anything above ten is going to deteriorate into something very much resembling doodling with many of your students. Even keeping the number down can't take much away from the monotony and meaninglessness of the task, especially for those students who have trouble with vocabulary and consistently misspell ten words or more per test. I'm inclined to believe the exercise does them little or no good at all. Try saving drill papers over the weeks and check to see how many of your students keep misspelling the same words over and over. I think you'll discover that drilling their mistakes seldom prevents students from making the same ones in a subsequent test. And how often have you seen a word misspelled on a student's paper and then misspelled again on his drill paper ten or fifteen or twenty times? If you make your students do drillwork, I'll bet you sometimes wonder why.

As a matter of fact, don't you occasionally even wonder why you give them a written word test once or twice or three times every week? It's possible, of course, that they wouldn't study if you didn't. But in all the years I have taught English, one thing that keeps bugging me is the increasing evidence that the vast majority of students who excel in vocabulary, by their own admission do not study it very hard—sometimes not at all—and most of those who have a great deal of difficulty with it, by their own admission also do not study it very hard—sometimes not at all. The body of students in between those two groups quite possibly would simply—because of their attitude, ability, and temperament— study it every week whether they were going to be tested on it or not. On my own, I once began a vocabulary testing program years ago with one of my classes, in which I administered only one test every six weeks—that being 100 words in length. Comparative test-score data based on the weekly testing technique versus the one-test-every-six-weeks technique seemed to be lending some credence to the validity of my premise. Unfortunately I was caught—rather early in the experiment—and discontinued the plan. (The threat of ten days in the electric chair is no small deterrent.)

Aside from that, the obvious advantage of reducing the number of vocabulary tests to six per year is that it would allow you the entire period once a week for discovering and solving a greater number of word-meaning and pronunciation problems among students. In addition, there could of course be oral spelling of the more troublesome words in the lesson. Weekly testing automatically precludes the possibility of more than a quarter hour or so for this kind of vocabulary exploration.

My students have been poles apart in their written comment on this phase of language study, even though you hope their year-end course evaluations will reflect some kind of consensus. Interestingly enough, though, most of what they say is directly related to the problems we have been discussing with regard to vocabulary learning. For instance, there are scores of comments pro and con about the workbook itself:

> "Vocabulary is a very important part of English, but not from a book where we learn words we knew in second grade."
> "Doing the workbook is the fun part but we hardly used it."

"Maybe if you tried a different workbook, or system, it might help."

"At 1.25 dallors for a workbook. We should at least wright in it."

"Vocablery or spelling or spelling workbooks bring to mind only one word: ICK!"

"Although I think it would of been more helpful to do the exercises in the workbook, I liked the way we did it."

Or on the teacher's approach:

"I thing you should spend more time on teaching the students the meaning of words then the spelling."

"You should be quieter during the tests."

"My last year teacher could show you how better."

"Why not let a different student give the lesson each week?"

Or on the course in general:

"Over all vocabulary was helpful, very good, and cannot be easily rapped."

"Of all the studies in English, this is the most useful."

"I didn't add any words to my vocabulary."

On that sad note it would seem wise to close our present discussion and get on to other things.

SUMMARY

1. The continued use of a workbook for vocabulary study in most school systems seems totally unrealistic.

2. Since your goal should be to teach all of the language, and time does not allow you to use the workbook the way it should be used, placing its written exercises on an optional status and requiring your students to use the dictionary approach, would seem as good an alternative as any.

3. Making the workbook optional precludes the necessity of your having to check each student's work every week. And if it is optional, then it follows you are just as well off without a workbook at all.

4. If you are still referring to this facet of your language program as "spelling," you are at least implying that word-meaning and pronunciation are of secondary importance. Students have to be constantly reminded that words whose meanings they do not know are of absolutely no use to them in their language. Terms like "vocabulary study" or "word anatomy" with reference to this part of your language program would seem to communicate the overall idea of what word study really is.

5. You really have only two options in the matter of testing. You can give the word-meaning-spelling type test or the spelling-only type test. Giving both types on alternate weeks seems a viable course to follow.

6. If you decide on the spelling-only type test exclusively, then considerable exploration of word-meaning through discussion before and during the test is of paramount importance.

7. Requiring students to drill their misspelled words seems a highly questionable practice, more than ten times for each misspelled word, terribly impertinent. A personal visit with you by each student to correctly spell the words he missed on his test would seem a wiser course.

8. You should leave open to possibility the giving of vocabulary tests only once every six weeks, still using that one day a week for oral exploration of meaning, pronunciation, and spelling of words in the weekly lesson.

6

Establishing a Diversified
Reading Lab

You know as well as I that among other things, literature teaching is a constant struggle against the temptation (often born of necessity) to build your program more or less permanently on what you have available in the way of reading materials. If available materials happen to consist of only a text or two, your literature program isn't going to have much going for it. Yet, I think many of us are faced with this kind of situation. So if we are to improve and broaden our literature study we have to explore new sources for materials, transcending the limitations of economics and/or the vagaries of school boards and administrations.

One very fruitful source is the paperback book club. Another is the classroom paperback library. Both can literally breathe life into your literature program.

Paperbacks and the Desire to Read

The fascination that the paperback holds for all young readers is in my view simply incredible. That is why literature pro-

grams at least partially based on paperback use would seem to
have considerably better chance of success than those which are
not. This is especially true with literature courses involving less
able readers. So many of what we refer to as reading problems
are fundamentally attitude problems, that any device which tem-
pers those problems has just got to be considered extremely indispensable. In my estimation, the paperback is that kind of
device. It has further value in that it appeals to every student
whatever his reading ability happens to be. That is why all my
classes belong to a paperback book club—if they wish to. That
last clause is important; the program has to be voluntary. But as
I have pointed out, the paperback has unbelievable appeal to all
students, and a high percentage of your students are going to
want to be a part of any club you sponsor. Your sponsorship of
one will make possible not only your own personal developmental reading program for problem readers, but will likewise
allow you to teach the novel, biography, autobiography, et cetera, to average and above-average readers. In addition, it can effect increased reading by the vast majority of your students and
give them a degree of pleasure in their reading that can't possibly come from conventional texts. Finally, it can make possible
the establishment of a personal card-catalogued paperback library in your classroom.

   Let's examine the latter three possibilities. First, the possibility of increased student reading: It seems fairly obvious that students voluntarily ordering books which they have chosen from a
list of forty or so, on their own individual order blanks, are doing so because they want something more to read. And that
"something" is not from a text in which you assigned a specific
lesson, but a book or books which have excited their interest.
Added to this is the fact *that they are ordering paperbacks.* The
evidence, then, presents itself rather forcefully that they are going to do considerably more reading than if they were not given
an opportunity to order through a book club. And as a matter of
fact, you can further enhance the opportunity with regular free
reading days on which they are encouraged to bring their paper-

backs to class. The second possibility—that of deriving greater pleasure from this kind of reading—follows *a priori*. As for the possibility of your developing a classroom library consisting solely of paperbacks, its realization is strictly up to you. If you want to take the action necessary, such a library will become a reality. In my room there is at present such a library, consisting of more than 400 volumes ranging from 4th grade reading level all the way through the adult levels. It is constantly in use. About half of the volumes are donations from students and myself. The rest have come through our use of the free dividend plan of our book club.

The accumulation of paperbacks for a library is relatively easy. Inform your students that you are beginning one for *their* use and that contributions of their already-read paperbacks lying around the house gathering dust would be appreciated. That is the way I put it to my classes several years ago. Response was just short of overwhelming; in the first week alone, our library expanded to nearly fifty paperbacks and grew by five or ten a week thereafter. Students still contribute substantially to it over each year. Added volumes through our book club are at present averaging over fifty a year.

If you build a library, it seems wise to card-catalogue it. The "in" and "out" system, using 3×5 index cards, is about as workable a method as any, and large numbers of students will volunteer as librarians. So here, then, you have another valuable resource which virtually guarantees increased reading by your students, and at every reading level.

However you acquire added reading materials, the more you have, the better are your chances of succeeding with your literature teaching—which observation perhaps appears to be a *non sequitur*, but which I believe to be a valid conclusion—provided you know how to best utilize any materials you have been able to acquire. For it is a fact that variety is of paramount importance to adolescents, and variety is one of the best weapons I know of for improving students' attitudes toward reading. It is also the great leveler with respect to varying reading skills. And student attitudes and skills occupy positions of importance in the teaching of literature that they occupy in no other area of language learning. If you give them the consideration they deserve, then I believe your approach to literature teaching is a realistic one.

Techniques: The Problem Reader

With respect to student skills it seems obvious that the more reading material you have access to, the better chance you have of accommodating all levels of ability in your classroom. For the "lower" end of the ability spectrum there are any number of anthologies published which are excellent from the standpoint of simplicity of approach. Unfortunately these same publications are frequently inferior (at least in part) with regard to subject matter, but you can't have everything and a perceptive teacher can get around this problem by simply being selective. Then there is dual-level text developmental reading, a technique specifically designed for slow readers. The dual-level text serves very well as a class leveler where within one group there are great differences in reading ability. But I think in terms of attractiveness and variety of subject matter, the student paperback book club is far and away the best thing going for the reader with low ability. It is economical, to say the least. That is a point in its favor. But its strongest point is that it makes available to your students the greatest possible variety of simplified reading materials and desirable (from their standpoint) subject matter. And of course it is equally attractive to average and above-average readers.

I daresay you have access to at least one anthology and perhaps more. As for a developmental reading lab, I would guess relatively few of you are familiar with this device. That would leave a good many of you "holding the bag" with recourse exclusively to no other literary resource but the anthology for use with your problem readers. But in your capacity as a teacher you can, with a little ingenuity and only some personal inconvenience, make the student paperback club serve your needs admirably. More about this later.

Conventional Developmental Reading

I should like to digress slightly to explain just a bit about developmental reading, which will be referred to later in the chapter in connection with paperbacks. If you have never used this approach in your classroom, I should like to begin by saying it is not at all difficult to teach. The developmental approach is, however, at times a drag to your students and you, but where low-ability readers are involved, it is well worth it.

The theory of a developmental reading course is that preselection preparation, segmented readings, and subsequent recall through discussion of the material read, are bound to improve a student's reading. The student must move along at a slow enough pace to allow maximum comprehension of what is being read, but not so slow as to disallow improvement in reading speed. Part of the mechanism of the developmental method is the dual-level text. Both texts cover exactly the same material, but not at the same level of language sophistication. One text is simpler than the other, but (theoretically, at least) neither is so difficult as to be beyond the reading ability of any of your students.

Most developmental reading labs include a workbook as part of the course. The lessons in it stress for the most part exercises in semantics and word anatomy along with unit tests on the workbook material. Otherwise, what you do in this kind of reading course is: (1) through preselection prepare exercises for the troublesome vocabulary you will meet in the selection itself, and some of the questions you are going to be asked after reading it, (2) read a portion of the selection, (3) digest what you have read through discussion of the material, (4) read and digest more of the selection, et cetera. With the supplemental material in the workbook, the course moves along at something akin to a snail's pace. This may lead you ultimately to the act of eliminating the workbook from your developmental course. The reasons for doing so, I think, will become apparent rather early. For one thing, the workbook is too often an entirely separate entity from the text, with no apparent connection to its subject matter. For another, doing all the workbook exercises occupies nearly as much time as the actual reading and discussion, making it in the long run too predominant an element in a course which I believe must be primarily a reading course—a fair assumption, it seems to me. Without the workbook your course moves along at a speed which is more compatible with student temperament and needs. Furthermore, I doubt that eliminating the workbook downgrades the effects of the course very much, if at all, since it is entirely possible to do much of the workbook kind of thing through class discussion under your leadership.

Throughout the course there are opportunities for student self-expression within group activities, as well as carefully selected bibliographies at the end of each unit of study to allow students to further explore the subject matter they have just been exposed to in the unit—whether it be fiction or nonfiction.

For low-ability readers I think the developmental plan is one of the few realistic approaches you have open to you. If your curriculum does not call for such a program, you might profitably look into the possibilities of bringing one into your school. It is an economical tool. One set of dual-level texts suffices for a room, since everything you do in connection with the course is classroom oriented.

There is no trick to teaching developmental reading. You need only exercise patience and perceptiveness—patience, because of the program's slow pace, and perceptiveness because you have to keep your eyes open during the timed-silent-reading periods to see which of your students are progressing well enough to graduate from the more basic text to the regular text, and which of your students perhaps have the wrong text to begin with. At the beginning of your program in the fall, a reading test is certainly in order to determine about where all of your students are in ability.

Make Your Own Reading Lab

Not only is the book club discussed earlier an added incentive for your problem readers to read more than they have ever read before, it makes available opportunities for them to acquire attractive reading material at levels compatible with their skills. Aside from this, however, you can even use the book club to build a kind of do-it-yourself developmental reading lab by taking advantage of the book-dividend system inherent in all book clubs to order paperbacks printed at whatever levels of reading ability you desire—from fifth grade all the way on up through high school.

Let's assume you have an eighth grade class of 30 whose reading ability begins at the fifth grade level and moves up to say, the eighth grade or average level. At dividend time you order sets of three different novels, one set for fifth grade ability, one set for sixth or seventh grade ability, and one set for eighth grade ability. Or as with some book clubs, the three levels might be "very easy," "easy," and "average junior high," respectively. Distribution of each set to the students with corresponding reading ability would be the next step, and *voilá*, you have the makings of a developmental reading program in which your students will be using more current and far more readable material than in a conventional developmental plan. In essence you have acquired a multiple-level, multiple-text reading lab.

As for specifics, divide each of *your* personal copies of the three novels into more or less equal reading segments. In keeping with the "short burst" theory of developmental reading, it is advisable to make each segment no less than six nor more than ten pages in length. The number of segments may vary. Any number between 10 and 30 may be used, depending upon how long you want to expose your class to developmental reading. In establishing segment lengths I have in the past simply timed my own readings of each book so that each segment is as close to six minutes as possible. The time-length at your rate of reading will of course be different. I don't know how fast I read, but I am no William Proxmire. Naturally, a six-minute segment at your reading rate will be considerably longer at most of your students' reading rates. In any event, you now have a "teacher's edition" to work with for each reading level. I think here I should remind you that when students are involved with this kind of slow-moving structured reading program, it is best to let them use both weekly literature days of your staggered schedule to somewhat accelerate the process. *But it is not necessary to finish whatever books you have chosen for your developmental reading program.* Even at these reading levels, 10, 15, and frequently 30 segments will only partially developmentalize the books you are using. As with the conventional dual-level text developmental reading program, you may stop at whatever point you wish and allow your readers to finish their books at their own pace on subsequent free reading days.

Suppose we take three novels on the current list of one paperback book club as examples to demonstrate more clearly what I'm talking about. Anne Emery's *Mountain Laurel* might be a good selection for that eighth grade reading level. It is listed as "average junior high." Robert Lipsyte's *The Contender,* listed as "easy," could well be suitable for sixth or seventh grade reading levels. And Robb White's *Up Periscope* seems appropriate for that fifth grade reading level—listed as "very easy." Now, let's assume that your class of 30 students, as established through testing and observation over the weeks, is composed of eight average readers, thirteen at the sixth and seventh grade level, and nine at the fifth grade level. You would order 8 copies of *Mountain Laurel,* 13 copies of *The Contender,* and 9 copies of *Up Periscope,* plus one copy in each category for your own personal use. Upon receiving the books, you would immediately proceed to segment your three copies for teaching and assigning purposes. It remains then only for you to hand out the paperbacks to your students, matching them with the appropriate student reading levels. The procedure from then on is as follows: Assign each group a segment at a time (beginning with the first, naturally) of their respective novels to be read silently in class each literature day. When you are sure everyone has finished his reading assignment, develop discussion covering the segments read within each group, moving from one group to another. *Keep your questions basic and summary-oriented.* If there is time, you might want to get some commentary from your students relative to the likes and dislikes for their respective books and why. But remember, one of the fundamental purposes of developmental reading is to improve recall and retention of facts through repeated short readings and discussions. Discussion should consume no more than 30 minutes total per segment for the entire class, or ten minutes per group. This is primarily a reading program. Even with abbreviated discussions, you will rarely manage to cover more than one segment during a literature period.

Yes, you are going to have to stay ahead of the class in your reading, but once you have read a book and drawn up discussion material for it, the job is finished once and for all. Each laboratory set stays right in the room and can be used over and over for other classes in subsequent semesters for as long as it lasts. As you acquire further sets, you of course have to go through the same process with each new set. Now, maybe you don't feel it is necessary to set up a developmental reading library using as many as three levels of material, though it is not actually such a formidable task. No problem there. Order only two different reading levels of paperbacks and follow the same procedure explained above. But make certain your lower level paperback is elementary enough to accommodate *all* of your problem readers.

It follows that in addition to the creation of a developmental reading lab, exploitation of the dividend system of your book club also makes possible the creation of a highly sophisticated group reading laboratory, which in time can serve all of your classes regardless of reading level.

Average and Above-Average Readers

What has already been said with respect to the paperback book club in general, and what it can do for your problem readers specifically, can in large part be applied to those of your students who have relatively few reading problems. But there are certainly things you want to do with your better readers—mostly in terms of quantity and sophistication of approach—that you can't do with your less skilled readers. This large group is academically capable of absorbing more literature (in varying degrees) and of course at more scholarly levels. The anthology comes into the picture here, too, but I believe it should occupy an extremely minor position. The kinds of junior and senior high school students we are talking about now, are, it seems to me, more than ready for the novel. If you do not have access to the novel within your school system, then again your book club solves the problem admirably. And I should like to suggest that the book club is a desirable adjunct even if your system does supply you with the necessary materials for teaching the novel. Efficient use of your membership simply increases the versatility of your novel-teaching library.

Group Reading

Your book club membership allows you also to build a group reading library which will accommodate as many small groups as you wish it to. In a class of 30 or 35, I should guess seven or eight groups is about all one teacher can manage with respect to individual panel discussions of the various materials being read. Five groups has proven the most manageable number in my classes. However, pick a number. Do you want ten or eleven groups of three, fifteen groups of two? Whatever works best for you would seem to be the ideal.

Let's try it with ten. Utilizing your staggered schedule, assign reading material to be completed over a week's time, announcing that discussion will take place based on: (1) study guide questions composed by the students themselves—three per student maximum, or (2) a paragraph analyzing one of the characters confronted in their reading, using the actions, utterances, and motives of the character as the basis for analysis, or (3) a written summary of the material read. A fourth alternative is one which all students enjoy and can profit from. It is called

"Who's Speaking?" In round-robin fashion each panel member reads short passages of dialogue from the assigned material, and in turn the rest of the panel members try to identify the speaker or speakers and the circumstances under which the words were spoken. The reader scores each student's correct answers on a tally sheet.

In addition to any of the above activities assigned, have your students compile a list of troublesome vocabulary they find during the week's reading. The last 15 minutes (at least) can be spent by the entire class in dictionary work, using their word lists as a study source. It is unwise, I think, to assume they will have consulted the dictionary as they came across such vocabulary in their reading, so you must require them to look up meanings on their literature day. Having them compose sentences in which they use each word correctly is perhaps as good a practice as any.

Perhaps you doubt the feasibility of students developing their own study guide questions. The majority of my students have demonstrated reasonable competence in this area, and as often as not, they come up with guide material that is as provocative as anything I might suggest. My advice to students in their formulation of guide questions is to first decide what is most unique about the book being discussed, and then to work from there. The simple proposition, "Is there a moral to this story?" in reference to Steinbeck's *The Pearl,* or "How would the author have been treated in the North?" in reference to Griffin's *Black Like Me,* might be two typical examples resulting from this kind of approach. What one member thinks is unique about a book is not necessarily going to coincide with what the other members of the panel think. This is what makes horse races—and lively discussions. With most seventh graders, you yourself are going to have to come through with assigned study guide questions at least the first couple of times. After that it is possible and I think desirable to leave them on their own. Students at this level—if allowed to—can develop the kind of material that is conducive to discussion as well as, and in some cases, more ably than their older colleagues.

Discussion based on the second technique—character analysis

—begins with each student on the panel reading his paragraph. Subsequent exploration of their similarities and differences in judgment can make for some very interesting exchange. This technique, incidentally, works extremely well with eleventh and twelfth graders. That is not to say it is unsuited for junior high school students. You can easily expose seventh, eighth, and ninth graders to this kind of writing in the composition phase of your program. By allowing them, in a laboratory environment, to do the same thing with characters in short anthology selections, you are in a position to teach them how to ask questions and come up with answers based on their words and actions. In this way, you make them better able to do this kind of writing for their panel discussions in literature.

Roughly the same procedure can be followed with the third technique. Each panel member reads his summary and through discussion the group tries to arrive at a consensus regarding the events which have transpired, concentrating on the contradictions that are most apparent in their reports. The summary approach is one which is perhaps more appropriate at the junior high school level, though certainly not out of the question in a senior high school situation.

All of the techniques presented here have value, and any discussion period can involve one or more of them. If one of the groups should come up with an unusual number of troublesome words from their reading, it is entirely possible you might want that group to spend the whole period on vocabulary exploration. If an especially cogent discussion based on character analysis is in progress, or a game of "Who's Speaking?" seems to be producing good results, then there is no need for you to switch the group or groups involved to some other discussion technique. Your approach, in other words, should be pragmatic. However, I believe it is of paramount importance that you set aside at least 15 minutes of every one of these discussion periods for vocabulary exploration.

Is it possible for several groups to carry on simultaneous discussions in the confines of one classroom? It is with some groups and at all levels of secondary education. With others it is a physical impossibility, mostly for reasons of student and teacher temperament. At least one teacher I know claims that the problem can be best dealt with by never letting it arise. "I have experimented with Babel and found it wanting," is the way she put it. If you feel strongly that discussions within a classroom environment are better conducted one at a time so as to be heard and participated in by everyone in parliamentary fashion, that is your prerogative. As always, the important thing is that idea exchange is taking place.

The system in which you teach is perhaps willing to invest in an "instant" group reading lab, and there are several publishing houses which have available classroom paperback libraries specifically designed for this technique. Holt's *Impact* series, published by Holt, Rinehart and Winston, 1968, is one of the better ones suitable for literature courses at the secondary level. But if you pursue your book club membership doggedly and select your dividends with prudence and foresight, it will not be long before you have a reading lab every bit as versatile as any you can buy ready-made.

Discussion

Even with your better readers you are not following a wise course if you pick student brains excessively about plot development in a given story, the author's style, et cetera. It seems to me with this kind of technique you are apt to quite thoroughly cancel out any enjoyment they have experienced in their reading by subjecting them to what very often turns out to be an unenlightening, stultifying experience. Adolescents (even the best of them) are not overly astute at commentary on plot. They know a good or bad plot when they see one (perhaps), but there aren't many of them who can expand to any degree on the character of its development and why it is a good or bad plot. As for conversing with them intelligently about any author's style, you are quite probably going to fail abysmally with every attempt you ever make in this direction. Style to an adolescent comes in little one-word or one-phrase packages labeled "funny" or "lotsa description" or "interesting" or "boring." Any attempts to get them to elaborate on their laconicisms elicit—except in rare instances—embarrassing incoherencies or blank stares. Obviously, this is truer of junior high school students. But I daresay, if you are teaching at the senior high level, you are thoroughly familiar with the kind of situation I have just described. If perchance your experience indicates the opposite to be true, then I heartily envy and congratulate you.

"What did you enjoy most about the story you just read?" generates as much intelligent commentary as you have a right to expect with this age group. Or, well into something like *Treasure Island,* a question, for instance, about who seems to be "stealing the show" so far, is a reasonable guarantee of some fairly lively discussion about Silver. In Steinbeck's *The Pearl,* a question dealing with the aptness of the book's title can lead to some very basic discussion about novels centered around things as much as people. Or with a selection like Hale's *The Man Without a Country,* the question, "Would you say this is fiction or non-fiction?" will invariably open the door to a discussion of why it reads like non-fiction when it is really fiction. Have you noticed how many of your students assume it is a true account?

The point is that discussion-oriented questions are hardly limited to the old standards. Every work of literature has its own distinctive characteristics, and the comments you make should bear as often as possible on these characteristics.

The Poetry Survey: Junior High School

Junior high school students—including seventh graders—with few or no reading problems are capable of reading two novels in the course of an academic year, plus whatever selected anthology pieces you pick and assign to them on the basis of curriculum requirements. The latter would, I should think, include a good deal of poetry, including an "in-depth" study of something in the nature of Longfellow's *Evangeline.*

Evangeline adapts particularly well to the reading habits of junior high school students if you point out to them that the poem can be read exactly as if it were prose. The poet's precise punctuation allows that. And even though they follow the rules for prose in reading it, it becomes increasingly evident the farther they get into the poem that its meter is inescapable.

As a rule, I believe it is important to allow your students to read virtually all their literature assignments silently. But with *Evangeline* there is good reason to make an exception. Try alternating cantos with them. They read one aloud, then you. And before you go into the study of *Evangeline,* find out how much your students know about metaphor and simile and alliteration. I'll venture they know little or nothing about these literary devices. Why not make your study of the poem the culmination of an investigation of all kinds of poetry forms. Keep your study, however, at a level junior high students can understand. Most of poetry's complexities are better dealt with later in their education.

In your poetry "survey," if we may call it that, use a simple approach, going through one or more of the literature anthologies available to you and reading the best of the poetry selections. Macmillan's *Currents in Poetry,* 1968, is one outstanding anthology available in paperback. Others, *Reflections on a Gift of Watermelon Pickle,* SBS, 1966, and *Cavalcade of Poems,* SBS, 1968, are available through book club membership. Comment briefly on the content of each poem, taking care to accept all interpretations as "valid." Move then to discussion of the poem's rhyme pattern (if it has one) and its meter; talk about its visual form, pointing out the tremendous diversification that poetry allows, perhaps reducing the lesson to terms of what your students might produce in the way of a poem themselves. The extent to which your study acquires any real sophistication will lie in your exploration of simile, metaphor, and alliteration, reaching a kind of grand climax in *Evangeline,* where your students will be literally bombarded with examples of all three forms.

You will discover to your delight that junior high school students seem to dig these literary devices. Ask them to ferret out any of the three forms in a poem, and you will be pleasantly sur prised at their perceptiveness. Once you have taught them what they really are and the purposes they serve in literature, your students will more or less take it from there.

Alliteration defined as "several consecutive similar sounds" would seem to suffice for that literary device. The dictionary definitions of metaphor and simile are as good as any—to begin with at least. Examples of each on the board are a logical follow-up. A quote from the late Martin Luther King is always good for openers. For instance, his "mountain of despair," explained as an emotion given concrete form, describes one common kind of metaphor. Repeating the concept of "implied comparison" helps relate the specific to the general. "Sweetheart" as another kind of metaphor which gives to something a property it is not ordinarily thought of as possessing, could be another example. Reinforcement of the concept through identification of examples in the poetry survey makes your students ripe for the metaphoric harvest they will reap in *Evangeline*.

Description by explicit comparison, often through the use of "as" and "like"—that is, simile—can be explained in the same manner, using examples and perhaps even reducing a metaphor to similic terms to demonstrate their differences.

At the conclusion of *Evangeline* try testing your students on their recognition of the three forms, giving metaphor priority over simile, and simile precedence over alliteration. Then have them look for the various forms from passages of the poems they have read, identifying metaphor first, then simile, only if there is no metaphor in the passage, and alliteration if neither of the other two are present. It's a good exercise in perceptiveness and I think the results will please you. You may score the test if you feel the need to, but handed back to your students, scored or unscored, it becomes an effective and entertaining vehicle for discussion.

Once you have gotten through the survey, the instances of these literary devices in student writing—especially metaphor —will very possibly show a significant rise. The metaphor will often be quite bad, but it at least indicates that your students are applying what they have learned to their own uses.

You perhaps have the same feelings about *Evangeline* that some of my colleagues have; namely, that it is a kind of hokey, maudlin poem with little appeal to adolescents. Call me square, but I think a lot depends on your approach to the work. It *is* somewhat hokey, but I can't go along with the "maudlin" part. If at the outset you tell your students it is hokey—and I do— you must qualify your observation with a statement about Longfellow's romanticism, that his poem is a love story, and that all love stories are hokey to some degree. Pointing out further that the story is an exact parallel historically to the kind of tragedy so common in today's divided world, can very possibly enhance its appeal for them. Whatever else could be said about the poem, it is nonetheless a beautifully constructed piece of narrative literature and a marvelous vehicle for the teaching of language concepts that relatively few students are familiar with when they reach your room.

The Poetry Survey: Senior High School

Senior high school students are ready for exposure to some of the technical language in connection with the study of poetry. However, there is no reason why a format similar to that described for junior high school literature courses cannot be followed in the senior high school poetry classroom. Macmillan's *Designs in Poetry*, 1968 and *Poems to Enjoy*, 1967, are two attractive paperback anthologies for a poetry survey at the senior high school level. *Reflections* . . . and *Cavalcade* . . . , mentioned in connection with the junior high school survey, are appropriate for senior high school students with lesser abilities. At the beginning of your exploration, the following handout can be of significant value in helping your students to better understand the metrical qualities of the poetry they study:

I—Meter and the Poetic Foot
    A—A foot in poetry has two elements, one which is accented, one which is unaccented.
    B—Examples:
        1. The *iamb* which produces the *iambic* foot: One unaccented syllable preceding one accented syllable.

Pronounce the word "de*part*" or the phrase "to *love*." Each example represents an *iambic* foot.

2. The *trochee* which produces the *trochaic* foot: One accented syllable preceding one unaccented syllable. Pronounce the word "*love*ly." It represents a *trochaic* foot.

3. The *anapest* which produces the *anapestic* foot: Two unaccented syllables preceding one accented syllable. Pronounce the word "inter*fere*." It represents an *anapestic* foot.

4. The *dactyl* which produces the *dactyllic* foot: One accented syllable preceding two unaccented syllables. Pronounce the word "*lech*erous." It represents a dactyllic foot.

II—Meter Types

A—Lazy lady (Dimeter: two stresses)

B—Sizzling in the sun (Trimeter: three stresses)

C—Won't leave that grille until she's done. (Tetrameter: four stresses)

D—Behold a cloud bank moving from the west (Pentameter: five stresses)

E—Alas, this visitor's a most unwelcome guest! (Hexameter: six stresses)

Line A consists of two trochaic feet.

Line B consists of three trochaic feet, with the ending unaccented syllable dropped.

Line C consists of four iambic feet.

Line D consists of five iambic feet.

Line E consists of six iambic feet.

III—Scansion: The examination of verse, foot by foot, to discover what kind of measures and meter it consists of.

I think this is about as much technical material as high school youngsters need to know and can assimilate, considering the amount of time they have to spend on the study of poetry. However, you may add "spondaic" and "pyhrric" to their vocabulary if you wish. Learning the outline and recognizing the various stress patterns and meter in the poetry they read will serve at least as an adequate introduction to some of the literature courses they take during their undergraduate work a few years hence. More importantly, however, this much knowledge about the characteristics of poetry can, I think, add to their enjoyment of it. Furthermore, once your students have become familiar with this material, the way is open for at least one other source of discussion than content. An assignment a week in which they scan in writing a couple of stanzas is excellent practice and becomes a vehicle for some lively and frequently protracted exchange over differences of opinion with regard to their respective prosodies—among other things. And as your survey progresses it is not long before your students are "listeners" to the poetry they read, even when they do so silently. At least one other side effect of this close an analysis of poetry's technical aspects will manifest itself in the poetry-writing phase of your composition program. Senior high school students, I think, are more willing to try composing their own verse if the mechanics of the form are not so foreign to them.

As for talking about the content of any poem I don't know how you can allow anything less than free interpretation by every member of your class—even with poems whose content seems to convey a reasonably direct message. In fact, there is nothing quite as eye-opening as a session with adolescents during which they are encouraged to give free rein to their ideas about what the poet means. This is true in junior high school as well as in senior high school. Therefore, it is not always desirable to follow the study guide which accompanies each poem in a given anthology, nor as entertaining.

Want to do something a little different with your classes? Take a poem like Robert Frost's "A Hillside Thaw," ditto enough copies for your students, but leave the title off. Let them read it silently and then ask for individual interpretations. Try the same thing with Langston Hughes's "The Negro Speaks of Rivers." And there are many others. Many of the poems of Emily Dickinson, Stephen Crane, and Wallace Stevens—with or without titles—make excellent grist for this kind of discussion.

As with the junior high school survey, the identification of metaphor and simile in senior high school is an interesting and useful practice. Chances are that a high percentage of students even at the eleventh and twelfth grade levels will not be terribly familiar with them. With this in mind, most, if not all, of the work done in this area should be carried out through discussion, just as with junior high school students.

The senior high school survey can culminate with some such work as Earle Birney's "David," [1] equally appropriate, by the way, for ninth grade. It consists of 46 four-line stanzas of rather elusive meter, but highly descriptive narrative. A poignant portrait of a mountain-climbing tragedy in which the narrator has to choose between two extremely unpleasant alternatives, "David" is a thoroughly engrossing vicarious experience in dangerous adventure for any teenager. The half sad, half joyous recall of the storyteller's exploits with his friend David, ending in the latter's death, give the poem a strangely ominous flavor. Its vocabulary is refreshingly vigorous, and much of it is challenging enough to create ample discussion for however long it takes to read. And it should be read aloud. The rules for prose reading can be followed in the reading of "David," just as with *Evangeline*. In fact, the poet's "indiscriminate" splitting of syntax in deference to poetic form, requires the reader to do so. The poem is not exactly replete with metaphor and simile, but there is a sprinkling of them there for the alert student to discover.

At the conclusion of "David" ask your students to comment in a paragraph or more on Bobbie's (the narrator's) choice of alternatives. Better still, develop discussion around it: How was he motivated to make such a decision? Was he justified in doing what he did? Do you think his emotion overcame his reason? In the face of his dilemma, what would you have done? Why?

I see no reason why twelfth graders cannot spend a few weeks in the study of *Song of Myself*. Edwin H. Cady of Indiana University includes Whitman's work in his paperback anthology *The American Poets 1800–1900*, Scott, Foresman and Company, 1966. It is an accomplishment just getting a poem of this mag-

---

[1] See Dunning, Lueders, and Smith's anthology, *Some Haystacks Don't Even Have Any Needle*, Scott, Foresman and Company, 1969.

nitude read in a classroom situation, and I would think that should be your primary concern. *Song of Myself*, too, should be heard as well as seen. Alternate the oral reading task between you and your students, dividing the poem's 52 "paragraphs" into sections and using an outline such as the following suggested by Carl F. Strauch:

1. Paragraphs 1–18, the Self; mystical inter-penetration of the Self with all life and experience.
2. Paragraphs 19–25, definition of the Self; identification with the degraded and transfiguration of it; final merit of Self withheld; silence; end of the first half.
3. Paragraphs 26–38, life flowing in upon Self, then evolutionary inter-penetration of life.
4. Paragraphs 39–41, the Superman.
5. Paragraphs 42–52, larger questions of life—religion, faith, God, death; immortality and happiness mystically affirmed.[2]

You, yourself, might then assume the role of reader for the first and fourth sections and spread the reading of the other three among your students. Discussion in terms of the division headings is possible and often enough quite productive, but certainly not necessary. Encourage your students to interpret the poet freely. Whitman is certainly not oblique, and most of your students will identify with him for that reason—and the fact that he is profound without being pedantic. They perhaps will not dig Whitman the mystic, but they will dig Whitman the man.

The techniques that Whitman uses to substitute for rhyme and iron-clad meter are also promising bases for discussion. The preponderance of the poem's passages fall into the following four categories:

- *Ditto-ness*—a second line reinforces the first in more or less like terms, as in paragraph 2: "Houses and rooms are full of perfumes . . . the shelves are crowded with perfumes . . ."

---

[2] Carl F. Strauch, "The Structure of Walt Whitman's *Song of Myself*," *English Journal* (College Edition), XXVII (Sept., 1938), 596–607. For a somewhat different approach, see James E. Miller, Jr., "*Song of Myself* as Inverted Mystical Experience," *PMLA*, LXX (Sept. 1955), 636–661.

- *Contradiction*—a second line contrasts with or denies the first line, as in paragraph 3: "Clear and sweet is my soul . . . and clear and sweet is all that is not my soul . . ."
- *Addition*—a second line or several consecutive lines supplement the first line, as in paragraph 4: "Not words, not music or rhyme I want . . . not custom or lecture, not even the best . . ."
- *Pyramiding*—a series of lines building to a climax, as in paragraph 24: "Walt Whitman, an American, one of the roughs, a kosmos,/ Disorderly fleshy and sensual . . . eating drinking and breeding . . ."

Assignments in which your students are asked to find examples of these techniques, once you are well into the poem and have stopped periodically to point them out, can serve each week as the basis for discussion during a part of the period. Following that, you can go on with your oral reading, pausing from time to time to answer questions about troublesome vocabulary or perhaps curious syntax. If you feel it necessary to administer a test at the conclusion of your survey, I would suggest it take the form of an essay in which your students comment say, on what they feel are the most significant differences between Whitman's poetry and some of the other poetry they have studied. Or you might present them with some such proposition as this: "Whitman has been called an evangelist by some. Based on your reading of *Song of Myself*, do you agree? If so, why? If not, why not?" Or—"If someone said that Whitman's constant reference to himself, and his frequent use of the personal pronoun 'I' in *Song of Myself* were egotistical, how would you defend the poet? Or wouldn't you? Why not?" Better still, forget the test and use these kinds of questions to develop discussion at the conclusion of the poem. It's more fun, and I believe it has much more intrinsic value to students. Ideas born through the reading of good poetry deserve sharing—over and over.

Teaching the Novel

I have never been accused of over-astuteness by my college professors in my understanding of the novel. I can read a novel and like it or dislike it without being able to compile a very long list of the reasons why. I know that its general theme is always about someone in one station of life trying to reach another (not always higher) station in life (ascent) ; that all novels have certain common characteristics; that all good novels contain the gratuitous incident; and that meaning in a novel is relatively unimportant. It can say yes, no, or who cares. The novel is never tragic in the sense, for instance, that drama is tragic; the novel operates within the frame of injustice, and it is stuck with morality, managing to effect outrage in the reader simply because the reader knows the motivation of its characters.

All of the above leads one to question how much of this should be injected into the teaching of the novel to junior and senior high school students. Experience has given me the answer: Not much. That is not to say it is the answer derived from your experience. Ascent and gratuitous incident are reasonably understandable to students even at the junior high school level if you present them in understandable language. And the latter can create some good discussion, so the more of it you can spot in a given novel, the better.

For example, in *Treasure Island,* one of the novels my classes study—but one which is eminently suited to seventh graders—you can point to John Silver's escape at the novel's close as an example of gratuitous incident, in that it is certainly a surprise development, but perhaps not necessary to the plot. But your students will almost always speak of the episode in terms of a Stevenson "cop-out," and that it is at best a disappointing development. "A gratuitous incident," you can counter, "is not infrequently a kind of cop-out. The important thing about Silver's escape is that it is somewhat unexpected and not absolutely essential to the plot. Or did Stevenson perhaps consider it essential? Why do you think he included it in the story?" And so your discussion begins.

Or in a novel such as Arthur C. Clarke's *2001: A Space Odyssey,* discussion as to how the crystalline monolith in part one is related to the opaque monolith further on in the story can become mildly exhilarating. You might even suggest that part one is not essential to the plot and probe the class for their opinions. Incidentally, I heartily recommend this novel for ninth through twelfth grade. It is the finest piece of science fiction I've ever read.

The techniques you use in teaching the novel will be determined not only by how well-versed you are on the subject, but also by how many of its technical aspects you think your students can grasp—and naturally by the grade level you are teaching at. But be realistic. If your students can talk intelligently about the novel at all, you should be satisfied. Adolescents, when they pick up a novel, are simply looking for a good readable story. If their expectations are not dashed in the reading of it, they say the novel was a good one, but they are hard-put to say exactly why. There is nothing strange about that at all. And to warm them up to their subject you are going to have to carry most of the weight of any discussion. It will be your questions and comments that generate and regenerate it, questions and comments—as stated earlier—which bear as often as possible on the distinctive characteristics of each work of literature studied.

Your average readers can easily handle one assigned novel; your better readers, two novels—that is, in addition to the anthology assignments stipulated in the guide and the poetry survey we talked about. This is a lot of assigned reading for any student, considering all the other activities connected with your language course. But I happen to believe you have got to let your students *read* in any good literature program. With your staggered academic schedule again coming to the rescue, they do indeed get to read.

A Novel per Quarter

If you were setting up a course of study with Stevenson's *Treasure Island,* to mention one possibility, it could be easily completed over a nine-week period with seventh, eighth, or ninth grade students, giving one take-home reading assignment a week. On their literature day give your students a short, summary-oriented quiz, after which a discussion, first in the context of the quiz they have just taken, and then using the simple specific question approach referred to earlier. The quiz tells you readily whether a student is doing his reading or not, but it also aids him if he has not. That is a valid reason for going through the test orally immediately after your students have taken it. The following might be part of one such quiz in a series of nine for *Treasure Island*:

Chapter XX Silver's Embassy

1. As the chapter opens (a) a ferocious battle is in progress (b) Silver and a companion are waving a white cloth just outside the stockade (c) Dr. Livesey and Smollett have undertaken a mission of peace to the enemy camp.

2. In the course of the talks that follow, Silver asks for (a) a 48-hour truce (b) the map, the treasure, and the Hispaniola (c) food.

3. In return he offers Smollett and his followers (a) a fair share of the treasure (b) Skeleton Island (c) ". . . my affydavy, upon my word of honor, to clap you somewhere safe ashore."

4. Smollett's anwer in effect is (a) conciliatory (b) a blunt order for Silver to leave the stockade (c) to hold Silver as a hostage.

5. Silver reacts to this by (a) thanking the captain (b) producing a hidden knife and fighting his way free (c) stumbling off, muttering a dreadful oath.

With the last such quiz, ask your students to react to the novel honestly in the confines of a paragraph of commentary. The following recent examples of this kind of commentary from some of my pupils may give you an idea of what junior high school students can do in the way of intelligent appraisal if you don't channel your assignments, thereby stifling their power of expression:

I think *Treasure Island* is a very good book. Both young and old can read it, understand it, and enjoy it. Its many climaxes kept the book exciting from beginning to end. The "pirate talk" made some parts of the book hard to understand, but not that much. It was easy to keep up with the characters, because there weren't too many. *Treasure Island* is the best book we have read all year.[3]

I liked the book *Treasure Island* a lot. All the characters seemed very real to life. I admired Jim because of his courage and his faithfulness to his companions. He had a lot of nerve to set the boat adrift. Long John Silver I also liked. Even though he was a buccaneer, he was different from the others. I think that Stevenson did an excellent job creating this book.[4]

Treasure Island was a good book, but I was let down by the ending. I thought it was too subtle. I would have preferred a more exciting ending for Silver. To have him come to blows with the Squire, or something of this nature would have been a better ending for him and the book.[5]

I did not like *Treasure Island*. The story is mainly dialog which was full of sailors' jargon. This was very hard for me to understand because I am not familiar with many sea terms. Also, the book is too old-fashioned. I don't see any need in assigning old books which don't appeal to the students while there are so many good up-to-date books available.[6]

The same procedure can be followed for any other novel your classes study. For instance, another of Stevenson's creations, *The Master of Ballantrae*, takes about the same period of time to cover as *Treasure Island*. Because of its strange format and somewhat stiff, pedantic tone, this novel is hardly suited for seventh grade students, but good readers in the eighth grade have no trouble with it. I believe its level of sophistication makes it suitable for use with ninth through twelfth grade students as well. There is considerable vagueness in this historical novel, and it is almost a must for you to go into some background research of the period, particularly of the Battle of Culloden, as much for your own edification as for the students'. The story's bizarre ending is guaranteed to create curiosity discussion with your classes. Students will ask all sorts of questions about tongue-swallowing, Indian (Asiatic) customs, and, "Are

---

[3] Julie Lange is the authoress.
[4] The authoress is Patti Milne.
[5] Pete Calkins is the author.
[6] Kathryn Schutz is the authoress.

there really guys like Secundra Dass?", "Why did Henry drop dead?", and "What ever happened to the buried treasure?". Here are some recent reactions to the novel from an upper track group of students:

The Master of Ballantrae seemed to me to be an artfully constructed novel. The author builds up to at least three minor climaxes and finally the grand climax only to lead you to a surprise ending. The ending seems to be a little letdown in excitement as the Master dies, but it ends with a bang as Henry dies. The book is easy to believe because of places and dates. At times the author makes you feel as if it really happened. He also develops each person's character to the fullest. Once he seems to build an image, though, he sometimes shatters it. When you thought you knew Henry, RLS changed his character by having him go insane. When you thought you hated James, Stevenson showed his human side. This was a well-written book.[7]

This book traverses from great excitement to utter boredom. It is enjoyable enough as you read it, but it's not the type you are apt to remember for a great while. In a sense, I think reading this book was a waste of time, because it seemed pointless fiction, interspersed with bits of entertainment. I would recommend a new novel for next year's eighth graders.[8]

The Master of Ballantrae was an extremely difficult book to stick with. Because of its slow start the book was like a chore. I never became deeply interested until the fascinating finish. There, Stevenson abandoned his slowness and came up with an exciting end. I would recommend that you keep on giving your classes this book. It can teach them never to give up once they've started a book because it may have a great ending.[9]

The techniques I have just described are used when the entire class studies the same novel, but this does not preclude the possibility of your carrying on the kind of weekly activities described in connection with group reading when several *different* novels are being read. The weekly quiz and teacher-led discussions, then, are not necessary adjuncts to your teaching of the novel; they only represent another approach.

---

[7] The authoress is Pamela Marquardt.
[8] Bruce Olson is the author.
[9] Tony Steiner is the author.

If you have never exposed your students to the study of the novel, I highly recommend it. Experience with it has shown me that the vast majority of adolescents beginning with seventh graders, much prefer it to any kind of literature anthology. I can think of nothing better than having a half dozen or so sets of novels always available in paperback on your book shelves. When one set wears out, order another set to replace it—a different novel if you choose. Financially, it can be most economical, what with the publishing revolution and the availability of virtually everything ever written in low-cost paperback form. And if you enjoy membership in a book club, it is possible to fill your shelves on a cost-free basis.

Free Reading

For lack of a more definitive name, we have designated one day every other week as "free reading" day. On this day all of my students (except those currently occupied with developmental reading) are allowed to spend the entire period reading the paperback of their choice, whether from the classroom library or from their own, with no interruptions from their teacher. If you put this kind of plan into your literature program, your only part in it need be walking quietly about the room watching for lip and/or head movement, and checking your extreme problem readers to make certain that they are not reading material way beyond their ability. If they are, your paperback library comes to the rescue. In correcting lip movement, a finger placed in front of the reader's mouth will suffice; to arrest head movement, firm but gentle pressure of the hands on either side of the reader's head will do the trick. Otherwise, it is as if you are not even in the room.

Does this kind of literature day appeal to adolescents? I assure you, no other phase of your course will receive as many accolades on the year-end student evaluations. In a recent year, of 101 evaluations which carried comments about the free-reading day, only three of them echoed dissatisfaction with it.

If my philosophy in connection with the teaching of literature seems oversimplified or unscientific, then I willingly accept guilt. I doubt that my powers of observation are much less than those of most other educators, and my observation tells me that students at every level of education will read if you just give them the chance. Even your slowest readers will read if you hand them a paperback, and if it is one which is written at their level they will read with a gusto you never thought possible.

If it could be said that the only legitimate goal of literature teaching is to give students a desire to read, then the course of action my students and I are following in our literature classes at present might be termed a modest success, if I am any judge of modest successes. Creation of desire to read, of course, is not the only goal, but if you could do something to help create it in some of your students, you'd feel pretty good about it, wouldn't you? In a manner of speaking, it's half the battle won. Once your students have the desire to read, it remains only for you to help them achieve greater skills in their reading. And the more ways you can find to create that desire, the more apt your program is to be a success. Does that sound more like a hunch than a fact? In education one must often trust a hunch and be guided by it, for education produces the intangible, which is the stuff of hunches. Many an educator stagnates for want of something more reliable to make him move.

SUMMARY

1. Today you need not be strapped with only one or two resources from which to teach your students literature. The most economical and easy-to-come-by addition to your classroom materials is the paperback. Paperbacks not only can add variety to your literature program, they can be instrumental in changing student attitudes toward reading—for the better.

2. With problem readers, one effective approach is the developmental reading technique, using the dual-level text to cover the same material. There are conventional dual-level text anthologies available through various publishing houses, but you can make your own

developmental reading lab by ordering paperbacks at various reading levels through your book club membership, and developing discussion material for each book.

3. With average and above-average readers at the junior and senior high school levels, the group-reading library—in which there are from five to fifteen different novels and/or biographies, autobiographies, et cetera—is an effective approach.

4. Simultaneous discussion by all the groups can be utilized where group temperament permits it. However, one group discussion at a time with the rest of the class participating can be just as effective.

5. Too much emphasis on discussion about plot development and such things as author's style would seem unwise with most adolescents. Rather, engage in discussion which concentrates on the special characteristics (uniqueness) of whatever piece of literature is being read.

6. The poetry "survey," culminating with *Evangeline* or some other comparable selection, is an excellent way to teach junior and senior high school students literary devices such as metaphor, simile, and alliteration. Such a literary work should be read aloud if students are to realize its full impact. In general, the teaching of poetry to junior and senior high school students should be kept at a level basic enough for all of them to understand.

7. The same general format can be followed at both levels of secondary education. However, at the senior high school level, students should be introduced to some of the technical aspects of poetry. In class discussions dealing with poetry, free interpretation of any poem by your students should be encouraged.

8. In teaching the novel, very brief, summary-oriented quizzes are useful in keeping clear in students' minds just what has transpired in the material

they are being quizzed on. The quiz, immediately after it has been administered, can become a lead-in to discussion. At the end of the novel, assigning students one-paragraph commentaries on any aspect or aspects of it can achieve some reasonably creative results. The discussion technique used in connection with group reading, referred to earlier, can be used in classes where the same novel is being read by all students. The weekly quiz and teacher-led discussion simply represent another approach.

9. Average and above-average students are capable of handling a great deal more literature than we sometimes give them credit for. It seems entirely feasible to assign as many as two novels to your better readers in addition to selections from anthologies and other sources, and at least one novel to your average readers.

10. The free reading day is a thoroughly attractive concept for both junior and senior high students. For those who neglect to bring reading material to class or who are struggling with a book beyond their ability, there is, of course, your classroom paperback library ready and able to serve.

7

The Value of Written
Student Course Evaluations

How seriously do you listen to your students? Do you believe they are capable of judgments about you and your course which can lead to better techniques, subject matter, and teaching in your classroom? Early in these pages, I emphasized the fact that I have listened to my students in the course of my teaching career. The emphasis was intentional, because during thirteen years as an educator at least one change in my teaching every year has come as a result of that listening.

The sounding board I use, and which has been most revealing, is the anonymous student evaluation. It is my students' last creation of the year and consists of one-paragraph commentaries on each of the five areas of the course. They are given their usual freedom of speech, but where there is to be criticism, they are asked to suggest alternatives. Of course, they don't come up with positive alternatives nearly often enough, but with sufficient frequency to make the project entirely worthwhile as well as entertaining.

You get suggestions like, "Instead of writing every week why dont we roost marshmellows in the school courtyard?" But you

168

also get such suggestions as, "Have you thought about studying paperback novels from our book club?" While the first idea is attractive, it isn't practical inasmuch as you don't have a barbecue pit in the school courtyard. The second idea has real merit and results in your doing just that the following year, after a little soft sobbing at not having thought of the idea yourself. In any event, you have listened to your students, and I for one rank the practice high up on the list of teacher priorities.

Students View Education Pragmatically

Most junior and senior high school students view formal education from an entirely different perspective than we do. Where ours tends to be monistic, theirs is pluralistic. They see education, among other things, as a boring, time-consuming, grade-oriented, but necessary means to success. It is a building jammed with others like themselves where they get preached at, meet friends, make enemies, have constant deadlines to meet, and begin another facet of their learning each time a bell rings. We see education largely in terms of achievement, or claim we do. So do they. Unfortunately, their definition of achievement is different from ours. Achievement to them is getting good grades—or not flunking. If in the process of getting good grades they have improved themselves intellectually, they are not noticeably convinced of it because they are preoccupied with that grade. If a student who is weak in vocabulary studies hard enough to get 100 on a vocabulary test and you congratulate him on having mastered X number of words, thereby augmenting his command of the language, he will likely be miffed that you emphasized that fact rather than the fact that he got 100. The 100 is tangible, achievement is not. Suggest to a student that his conscientious application to every writing assignment over the year has helped him to know himself better, and he might very well pooh-pooh the idea, especially if he averaged "C" in that phase of the course.

Now, I think it can be stated categorically that because of their attitude toward education—particularly as regards grades

—we as teachers doubt very much that adolescents can make an intelligent statement about, or evaluation of, education or any phase of it, because we feel they just don't know what the real goals of education are. The fact is, whether they are aware of "real goals" or not, many of them nevertheless can comment intelligently on a program they have been intimately involved with for ten months. Besides, what is so strange about their attitude? In the first place, where did they get the idea to begin with that grade is king? It's not hard to answer that one. From us, of course. Most of us imply as much. Nay, we insist! How could students possibly have any other viewpoint? Virtually everything they do in school is considered valuable or useful in terms of a letter or a number. In the second place, if they don't know why they are being educated (which I doubt), whose fault is that? Isn't it part of our job to make them understand why? Could we perhaps make them understand better if we de-emphasized or abolished grades? If we livened up our classrooms? If we occupied them with fewer meaningless tasks, or none at all? Well, my friends, if you listen to your students, these are all the things they are asking for. Not only that, but if you listen carefully, you will more than just occasionally hear words of wisdom.

Constructive Criticism

Some time ago I read this comment on a student evaluation: "The composition work was alright, but it wasn't time enough. I think we should of had two days of writing instead of one day. I sure could use the extra time." At the time, we were studying grammar for the entire period on one day and writing for the entire period on the next. Because of that one remark and the persistent appearance of others like it, we eventually abandoned the grammar textbook and went to our own writing for the study of syntax, cutting the time down to 15 minutes a week. That gave us a total composition time of 95 minutes spread out over two days, instead of the 55 minutes of one day we had been spending on writing up until then. And there is little doubt in my mind that since the adjustment, composition work in our classes has improved measurably.

"To me vocabulary is unnecessary. Learning to spell and learning the meanings of words both fall under literature. It may help the people who don't read much but I figure if a person doesn't care enough to read, he or she won't care enough to study their vocabulary."

"As far as I'm concerned, there must be a better way to learn vocabulary than to use a spelling book. One alternative might be to incorporate vocabulary right into the writing phase of the course."

The course evaluations I get echo such sentiments over and over. Just as frequently they contain this general idea: "This was really a boring part. It wasn't mind-bending at all. We just wrote down a bunch of words at the beginning of each week. And sometimes we had to work out a spelling chapter. I don't even want to write about it anymore." And: "This subject could be improved upon. Throw out that dumb spelling book. It is fine for the elementary grades; skip it in junior high. In its place should be reading selections in which the grammar structure and words are studied carefully and then ask the student to rewrite the selection using words with substitute meanings. Also issue bi-monthly sheets of higher-level spelling words to be learned. Words like 'print' and 'trader' in our present study don't add much to our vocabulary."

All four of those comments imply that vocabulary is not nearly challenging enough—or interesting—and are valuable for the reason that they are specific. Three of the four have added value in that they suggest ways in which it could be made more so. I think they give any English teacher pause for thought.

The suggestion that more emphasis be placed on word meaning in the study of vocabulary occurred no less than 26 times on class evaluations in a recent year. The episode inevitably led me in the following year to do just that—place a great deal more emphasis on word meaning in vocabulary study.

Negative Comments

Although constructive criticism in an evaluation is always the most desirable, non-constructive criticism can have value if it occurs frequently enough. In a survey of evaluations four years ago, I discovered there were many more negative than positive comments about the literature phase of my program—a phenomenon generally precipitated only by my grammar teaching. That same year the following comment in the alternative category appeared on one of the evaluations:

> "Paperbacks are neat. Why don't you save up are
> free dividends and get a set of scince fiction for are
> class? I'll give you mine."

There were two or three other suggestions similar in substance in the same batch of evaluations. Translation: (1) I apparently was not reaching my students with the approach to literature teaching I was using. (2) I was being offered a way out of my dilemma. I took the alternatives to heart and have never been sorry I did so. In short, the anonymous student evaluation forced me to take a good hard look at my literature teaching because of massive adverse student reaction to it, and further, offered an attractive alternative which I subsequently put to use. Since then, negativism with respect to my literature programs has declined significantly.

Down through the years, student evaluations have reflected an almost universal distaste for the study of grammar. I willingly confess that it is this fact more than any other that has influenced my attitude toward the teaching of syntax as a separate entity in an English classroom. But even with the drastic changes I have effected in my approach (for the better, I like to think), comments on year-end evaluations still manifest almost overwhelming dissatisfaction. Even 15 minutes exposure to it per week appears to be too much for some students:

> "Try to keep the students attention and try to make
> the material more comprehendible and not so unin-
> teresting."

"Now when I go to ninth grade I can tell the teacher I didn't learn anything."

"Language analysis wasn't really so great, I don't think it is really neccessary in some cases, I could go so far as to say, that it wasn't really worth while."

"Grammar has no real value and you know it."

"It's just as dumb in foreign language."

"I'm going to be a car machinic, boy will grammer help me!"

Just a few comments gleaned from past evaluations, and each year well over 50 per cent of them contain the same kind of negativism. For example, in this year's survey, of 162 comments in all with respect to grammar, there were 50 of a positive nature, 24 alternatives, and 88 of a negative nature. In cases like this, how can you *not* listen to your students?

Positivism

Of course, positive comments have their place too. If you find repeated approval of any phase of the course, consistently distributed throughout all your classes, you can legitimately assume, I think, that you aren't doing your job half badly—with reservations, of course.

In all the years that we have emphasized oral composition in our classes, the practice has elicited an unexpectedly high percentage of positive comment. I say "unexpectedly" because during the year students often refer to the oral presentation in such terms as "a trip to the gallows" and "the waiting game." From our most recent evaluations:

"Now, at the end of the course, I can get up and give my talk loudly, clearly, and without one goosebump, and I must say that is quite an accomplishment."

"For oral reports I was afraid because I thought that when you went up in front of the class everyone would stare at you. Now at the end of the year, I don't even think of it. They do stare at you, though."

"In oral composition I've learned to organize reports in a better way by having a limited amount of time to give them."

"It gives us a head start to speech in two or three years."

"The whole class gets to participate and say what they want. Even adults don't get to do that very often."

"Everyone listens to one another, since we all have a mutual respect for each other."

By listening to my students, I have discovered also that practically all of them approve of their writing regimen:

"The composition part of the course was excellent except for one area where we had to write about God, Faith, and sunrise and sunset, etc."

"This course did help me to learn how to write creatively."

"Composition equals creativity. This is the best part of the whole course, because everyone can do it."

"It's not dull or boring, but keeps your mind at work."

"This was the first English course of mine that deeply penitrated composition, how come?"

"Doing your writting all in classtime is great. That means know homework."

"To create a poem or a short story or even a theme out of nothing makes you feel proud."

But then there has never been any doubt in my mind that students at any grade level like to express themselves.

Instead of . . . How About . . . ?

As might be expected, the evaluations which manifest positive thinking are the ones which most often contain suggested alternatives. That is, even though students may express approval of some part of your program, they nevertheless come up with suggestions for further improvement. For example, how are these for possible alternatives in the literature phase of our course?

> "But I would think the students would like a little more to say in what they read. A suggestion may be: Hand out a sheet of paper with a list of books on it at the beginning of the year and the students could mark their first, second, and third choices and include ideas of what they are most interested in reading."

> "First quarter: Various short stories by different authors. Second quarter: Two novels, each very different. Third quarter: Poetry, ancient, classic, modern. Fourth quarter: Miscellaneous. Use every kind of materials available."

> "I think a new choice of novels should be found. Perhaps a Mark Twain story would be an interesting choice, because they're easy and fun to read. Also you might want to try a good science fiction. Keep *T. I.* but can *Master of Ballentrae.*"

> "For instance, since the movie 'Romeo and Juliet' came out, we realize that this story is still relevant. I found Shakespeare's writing beautiful and somewhat of a social comment. I think it would have been interesting to read and discuss this in class."

> "In this changing world I feel a modern novel or commentary on social conditions would have been far more valuable. A book like *A Raisin in the Sun, To Kill a Mockingbird,* or *But Not Next Door* would have made kids think."

Now, when you find eighth grade students who are capable of comprehensive, detailed, thoughtful remarks like this, you almost wish they were on the school board, or at the very least working on this year's curriculum committee.

Entertainment

Well, if you have carried on this kind of student-teacher relationship at the end of each year of school, you are aware of its possibilities as an effective liaison. You are also aware of its entertaining aspects—particularly with regard to humor. When you insist on anonymity, students tend to let their hair down, and all sorts of character traits manifest themselves in their writing. Not the least of them is blunt humor. Hardly any of the funny things you come across in these evaluations are intentionally humorous, which is what gives them their charm, and some of the humor is terribly uncomplimentary, so you have to gird yourself in the armor of humility and take up the papers with an open mind. Once you have done that, you are ready for salvoes like the following:

"Since it is the end of the year, I can truly say *I hated everything.*"

"The problem I have with writting is putting my thoughts down on paper."

"Writting stories is good because you get to know how to write stories."

"Oral presentations will help me in the future to face other teachers like you."

"Book reports weren't to bad because it was possible to get the information off the inside of the cover."

"Oral compositions in this course were fun untill it was my turn, by the time I go up in front of the class I decided I didn't like what I had in my notes. So I made it up as I went along. It sounded like I made it up too."

"The English language is sure messed up, isn't it?"

"I do want to say though that using the grammar sheets you gave us was easier than learning it. One question though—why do they want grammar taught?"

"Grammar was not interesting. This was boring. But it is necessary so I put up with it."

"I suppose that people should know what the parts of speech are but I don't think the modifying phrases are going to help you."

"After all, how many times in everyday life do you take a sentence apart and analysis it?"

"I think that language analysis could not have been done so poorly even if they tried. First we learned about S V DO ect. Next year we must learn NP VT ect. There is a wasted year on S V DO. Last year we learned about adj's and adv's and I knew what they were. This year I don't know what in the heck they are."

"Language analysis got to be a bore for some but for others it got even worse, not to mention any names. It really wasn't that bad but it could make you sick to your stomach."

"Grammer this year was fun. I didn't understand it at first but got the hang of it about May."

"Once you have learned basic grammar, you are ready for the funny farm."

"I think you should give us grammer only as a punishment."

"If you did not even touch on the subject of grammar, I would be no worse off."

"Vocabulary was auful if you didn't study."

"How come we have to learn how to spell potash?"

"Spelling was the worst day of all because you talk so much."

"Literature is very boring and undergoeing a great rejection from me through the most part."

"Evangilane striked me as rather boring. You liked it though."

"I no what you are thinking after you have read this, and your right, I hate the whole mess."

Entertaining or not, a number of these comments are eyeopeners, to put it mildly. The one about the "wasted year on S V DO" certainly reveals the ability of even adolescents to recognize the impractical aspects of trying to keep pace with constantly changing grammar-teaching systems. "The English language is sure messed up, isn't it?" quite possibly is referring in another way to the same problem. A remark like "After all, how many times in everyday life do you take a sentence apart and analysis it?" is devastatingly pragmatic, and any answer you give to it I think is going to have to be a snow job. And I'm not sure I know why "they" have to learn how to spell "potash."

It is precisely this pluralistic perspective of language study that adolescents have that makes their comments worth listening to. If they never suggested a constructive alternative, their evaluations would still have significance for teachers *because they are another means of communication*. Besides, our students see us and our course in a way we couldn't—not possibly. Through them we can look at ourselves and our teaching more objectively. What we hear from them is sometimes pleasant, but often something less than that. However, if we listen, we are no longer alone in that all-important process of periodic self-examination spoken of earlier. If we listen, there is a good chance we may learn something. If we listen, I think we lessen the danger of ever taking ourselves too seriously. In short, if we listen to our students, we are utilizing what I believe to be one of the few valid sources of teacher evaluation in education today.

So, listen here, teach' . . .

SUMMARY

1. Good language teaching demands that we listen to our students. No more valid source for teacher evaluation that I know of exists in education today. An effective way to tap this source is with the written student evaluation of your course at the end of the year.

2. The differences between students' views and our views of education are precisely what make their comments about it or any phase of it so valid for us.

3. Constructive criticism of your course by students is naturally the most desirable, and the least manifested in their evaluations. When it appears, however, it can as often as not result in a change for the better.

4. A specific negative comment, if it occurs often enough in a given number of student evaluations, can have its positive effects as well. If enough of your

students are disgruntled about some one aspect of your program, the cause for their complaint is certainly worth looking into with a view to possibly correcting the situation which brought it on.

5. Student evaluations reflect universal disenchantment with grammar study. Most of the comments made about it are negative, but their value is reflected in their frequency of appearance on evaluations.

6. If your students repeatedly voice approval of some part of your course, you can assume (validly, I believe) that you are at least headed in the right direction with regard to whatever phase it is they are commenting on.

7. Not infrequently, you get suggested alternatives from students regarding either techniques or the curriculum content of your program. These can be extremely valuable and often show remarkable creativity on the part of students.

8. From the standpoint of entertainment alone, the habit of listening to your students through written evaluation is well worth the trouble. No school year will ever go by without your having had many a chuckle reading their candid appraisal of your academic offerings.

8

Sparking Students to Their
Top Creative Levels

I suppose most of you find yourselves periodically wondering, as I do, what you can expect of your students with respect to creative productivity. Well, I think you can expect a great deal more of them than you probably do, both quantitatively and qualitatively, provided your interpretation of creativity is not too narrow.

At the outset, may I point out that my definition of creativity is a rather loose one. When I speak of creativity, I have in mind that activity of a student which requires him to take a task in hand that calls for ingenuity (whatever he possesses) as well as industry (however much he is capable of), the end result of which is something he can refer to as solely his own.

Now, that is broad indeed. Yet, how can it be otherwise? If you try to define creativity too narrowly, you tend to overlook the student's viewpoint: If you regard a piece of art or writing some student has done, for instance, as "uncreative," you automatically eliminate him from the whole act, which was all his in the first place. We keep saying creativity is relative and then often proceed to violate our own premise. Whatever a student produces which *his* ingenuity and industry have stamped "solely mine," it seems to me, just has to be creative. The "to whom" is incidental, except when "whom" refers to the creator.

Considering creativity in this light, how much of it are your students capable of? Unlimited amounts, of course. We need scarcely pause before giving the answer. Indeed, if in the course of their formal schooling, maximum emphasis was placed on the exploitation of their creative powers in *all* the subject areas, they would have barely scratched the surface of their potential. And that potential fairly cries for fulfillment in their pursuit of language mastery where the opportunities for it are so evident. So there remains little question of *how much* creative activity your students are capable of; the potential is there. There remains only the question of *the level at which they create.*

The Single-Paragraph Composition

What level of sophistication can an adolescent in secondary education begin writing at? What level can he reach? Any attempt to answer these questions has to be made in terms of the student's innate ability and his previous experiences with the language, and more specifically with language manipulation. In the area of creative writing you must assume that whatever experience he has had before entering your class has been largely haphazard and often inconsequential, unless you are teaching in an exceptional school system.

If at the first grade level he had jousted with language manipulation frequently and regularly in some kind of developmental sequence and continued the practice through the elementary grades, there is no telling what he could do by the time he reached you. Alas! It is in the realm of possibility that we will never know. But, as things stand, it has grown increasingly apparent to me that at the beginning of the fall term most junior high school and very probably senior high school students are in need of practice in organizing and unifying their ideas into that cohesive thing we call a paragraph. So that seems to be a logical starting point.

Now, I am acquainted with at least one educator who claims there is no such thing as a paragraph, a suggestion which leads me to believe that he would just prefer to call it something else. Yet, when I watch some of my students in their struggles to put one together, I'm inclined to believe the gentleman may have something there. I fight the idea, however, saying over and over to myself, "Yes, Tom, there is a paragraph," and conclude that it is probably the only realistic level at which you can start an adolescent writing if you are not to lose him at the outset.

Consider for a moment the following:

My boyfriend and I were walking on a damp, soft stretch of grass. Green, soft, a little damp. We see a tiny lake with some ducks diving for food on it. Along the shore of the lake there was the stump of a tree. My boyfriend and I go to the stump. We sat on it. Well my boyfriend did, but I missed. After getting up with the help of Bill who was laughing at the time beyond belief we went back home to see each other tomorrow.

Does the halting, laborious, spasmodic style look familiar? Though there is evidence the kind of student who wrote this is not half bad at developing a simple descriptive narrative, and even imbedding a sentence rather well here and there, to start her out with full-blown compositions involving descriptive detail and dialogue would obviously overwhelm her. She needs first of all, rudimentary instruction in tense formation and consistency, combination, punctuation, word choice (especially verbs), and probably more than anything else, proofreading—all in the confines of elementary one-paragraph assignments. If by the end of the year she is still laboring with single-paragraph development (the possibility is there), you can expect only that her paragraphs will perhaps flow more smoothly and show evidence of having been checked more carefully for errors on the final draft.

At least a quarter of my students every fall are at this level or below it, and I would guess the figures would be about the same for you. Ranging over the other three-quarters, the scale runs from mediocrity to excellence with every possible shade in between the two.

The following prose and poetry compositions—somewhat beyond mediocrity and in some cases approaching excellence—I hope, will help support my premise that writing adolescents are capable of almost unlimited creativity. Given enough opportunity, latitude, and the right kind of help, they come up with remarkable creations.

In making selections for this anthology, I chose what I considered to be the most representative of all my students in each phase of their writing program. Naturally I tried to pick the best in every case—from the standpoints of good writing and entertaining reading. There are many others I could easily have included, but had I chosen all of them, Chapter 8 would have approached interminability.

The single paragraph, as I have tried to point out, is not only a strategic starting point for your students, but an adequate vehicle for their self-expression. They write long paragraphs and short paragraphs, but almost invariably they get said what they want to say within its confines, whether it is long or short.

The paragraph you are about to read is certainly diminutive. I'll leave it to your judgment whether or not the author has shortchanged his reader:

Change the Subject

Tim was embarrassed when his friend asked him the difference between a square and a rectangle. Not knowing, Tim said, "Well, if you don't know, I'm not going to be the one to tell you." Tim lifted his head and looked to see if his friend doubted him. "I don't think you know either," his friend said. Tim looked up nervously. "We've had pizza twice this week at our house," he said. With that he turned around and walked home nonchalantly and left his friend standing there.

—*Ed Janecek*

Would you say the young man who wrote this is imaginative? I considered him as such, always expecting a half-humorous, very readable development of some simple premise, as in the above, and a good share of the time getting it. Incidentally, the impetus for this particular assignment was a given first sentence from which the student was asked to develop a composition of one paragraph. The nature of the sentence was obviously conducive to narrative, and the young author was consistently good at narrative. Strangely enough, beyond a single paragraph he was nowhere near as effective, preferring rather to do a thorough job on a smaller package. In other words, he had found his niche in single-paragraph composition.

Early in your writing program you hope your students can at least begin to grasp the fundamentals of descriptive detail—even if the end product is almost cold with objectivity. But there are always those young writers who manage to superimpose their own character over whatever detail they set down, virtually from the beginning. The superimposition is called style. Luckily, some arrive in your class already equipped with it:

Friends

Huddled together in their own dark corner of the hall closet are my Cossack boots. They stand at attention—tall, straight, and proud. My shiny black boots are always ready for one of winter's many adventures, whether it is to be tobogganing, skating, snowballing, or just a leisurely stroll to the bus stop. They're tough, yet as pliable and soft as a comfortable slipper. Their furry gray lining is useful because it protects me from moisture and frosty temperatures. To me, they are reliable old friends, for they have helped me to enjoy winter more.

—*Beth Goodson*

My Most Prized Possession

I stole softly into the room. It was extremely dark, but I knew that I wasn't alone. There were many stuffed animals peeping out at me from their respective corners where they had been flung earlier in the evening. As I crawled into bed I glimpsed two round, black objects on a gleaming white background. Immediately I knew that it was the muzzle of my stuffed donkey, Sprite. My imagination went to work, and soon I had a perfect picture of him in my mind. The happy red mouth, the bee on his nose, the floppy ears—everything was there. Yet, there seemed to be something missing. Could it be his eyes that were wrong? Yes, his eyes didn't seem quite as, well, cheerful as usual. Then, as a terrible feeling of guilt swept over me, I sprang out of bed in such a hurry that I tripped over one of my other animals. I murmured my regrets and scrambled to my feet. I rushed over to Sprite, hugged him, and hopped back into bed with a clear conscience. Sprite was happy again.

—Nancy Clark

The above—products of the first writing assignment of the year—are examples of the kind of creativity that helps to get your program off on the right foot. You keep your eye on the Beths and the Nancys for the rest of the year.

Have you found, as I have, that some adolescents possess a profundity of thought not found in many adults? How many of us could express as much in so few words as this:

There Is

Take a look around you; look at the trees, the grass, the animals, and the deep blue sky. Look at the green water, the graceful sea-gulls flying, the fish playing in the water, and the big, hot sun blazing over you. Alright, now walk until you hit the hustle and bustle of the city. See all the people; take a closer look. Watch them walk, talk, and breathe. Think of yourself, of all the things your body can do. Think of life and death and light and darkness. Sit down and let all these things whirl around in your head. Now, I ask you. Do you think there is a supreme being? There is—His name is God.

—Debbie Bartlein

The assignment which prompted this bit of reflection was extremely broad in nature. It occurred in the "concept development" segment of our writing program. The instructions stated simply that the student was to develop a paragraph relating in some way to the concept of God.

Whatever this young lady wrote for me always ended up the same kind of simple, warm prose that you see here. Her kind comes to you writing reasonably well, and leaves, hopefully, at least fortified with a desire to do even better things with the language in the future.

Not infrequently, adolescents bomb their English teachers with what I call the "quickie." Receipt of this kind of diminutive expression seems to justify your not specifying numbers of words in your assignments. As a matter of fact, it is one of the joys connected with teaching writing: It is often provocative and takes so little time to read and evaluate. The following is a fairly representative example of the "quickie." It is a product of the same assignment that produced Debbie's "There Is":

Operation: Concept God

If God is developed and shaped by each mind, then why is worship of him carried out in groups rather than individually? The worship of God wasn't meant to be carried out publicly nor does one God fit all people. If each person had his own little private altar or shrine, I think we could really carry out the true meaning of worship.

—Karen Dawson

A little imperious perhaps—but you'll have to admit Karen has managed three very pithy, interrelated statements.

And consider this diamond in the rough:

Eating Is Where It's At

They speak of protests and pot parties and drugs as being groovy. About the grooviest thing I can think of is food. Roast beef and potatoes turns me on. I freak out over steak and salad, puddings and pies, fruits and vegetables. Put a German chocolate cake in front of me and I'll go on a trip the likes of which has never been seen before. As far as I'm concerned, the drug scene is a dud, baby, because food is where it's at.

—Sandy Buchberger

Single- or multi-paragraph or narrative with dialogue were the options in the assignment that produced this paragraph. The area of our writing course in which it occurred was "human activities." Most obvious in this piece of writing is that the young lady gets down to the business at hand so readily. Notice the choice diction: the precise nouns and vigorous verbs.

Sandy's writing was most often characterized by its laconic quality. If she could make her point in a paragraph, she would do so, if the assignment allowed her the option. With luck, her brand of writer will visit you once every three years. Give her kind the germ of an idea and she's off and running with the effervescence of youth—plus one ingredient, an innate ability to entertain her reader with virtually everything she writes.

If you will, take a careful look at this next student creation. The young lady who wrote this had as much native talent as any student who has ever passed through my room:

Sleep

Looking up at the ceiling, waves of purple sweep around me. It's as if I was in a glass dome and a giant was pouring paint on it. Every now and then there's a hole in the purple and a startling green shows through. This always happens when I am just about to drop off to sleep. I close my eyes and see a pattern of red dots on a green background. My thoughts wander and then my subconscious mind takes over. I am spirited away to places beyond belief. I have adventures so fantastic that I can't remember them until sleep takes over again. I relive my past and sometimes there is a weird change in events. When I wake up, my adventures lie behind secret doors in the corners of my mind, and sleep is the only key that unlocks them.

—Kathy Maly

Another assignment in the "human activities" segment of our writing program, each student limited to a paragraph. The comment I put on this composition when I returned it was probably inadequate. From the standpoint of conciseness, clarity, diction, and descriptive detail, I think it is superb for an adolescent. It is something to move about the room and happen onto this kind of creativity in progress. The authoress left before the year was out, and I remember how disappointed I was to lose her.

Not many years ago there was an assignment in our writing unit that called for expository treatment of the following concept: "Through my formal education I am learning how to learn." It has since been replaced. But the year in which we used it produced some good things in all areas of our unit, and this area was no exception, as the following paragraph I think attests:

Learn How to Learn

In the course of being educated, a person is expected to do more than just listen and learn. He must learn how to use what he has learned and find out as much about what he is learning as he can. This takes extra work, which most people, including myself, do not wish to put forth. A person must develop good study habits, a memory, and an intelligence to grasp what bits of knowledge he may be offered. These tools that he must develop will be used all his life to broaden his understanding of living. A person shouldn't be satisfied with knowing there was a Civil War. He should want all the reasons and be willing and able to find them. If you don't learn how to find out the answers on your own, your life will be an empty existence, without pleasures you might otherwise experience.

—*Bruce Olson*

It perhaps would seem redundant to mention that Bruce was unusually mature for his age. And he was always just as business-like as his writing suggests—manifesting a bit of wry humor on occasion. What I remember about him most, however, is that he was red-haired, taller than average, and he had found his niche in expository writing—which he excelled at.

"Time Is Only Place." Some years that title suggests almost unlimited possibilities for students; other years it falls flat. But it keeps turning up periodically in our writing unit to produce some pretty enigmatic but intriguing prose. I think a couple or three readings of the following is called for:

Time Is Only Place

Time, the endless place. It's a stretch of nothingness only symbolized by my memory. I am sitting here alone, blind to the colors of the world, in a place that I am not yet familiar with. I feel as though I have died and time and my memory are my only friends; just sitting doing nothing, feeling it go on and on. I think to myself, "Will I never get out of here and feel as though I am living again?" But no, I tell myself, this is a place that cannot be escaped. I know that time is my jailor forever, forever, forever.

—*Cathy Wember*

I can't say why, but Miss Wember's interpretation always grabs me, no matter how often I read it.

Although Cathy's treatment was single paragraph, the nature of the title, I believe, requires that you give students full latitude in its development—including the option of verse.

One of the first items we ever used in the concept development segment of our writing unit was "reality." I have to confess that it seldom produced anything out of the ordinary in the way of student composition, but I saved one diminutive, though impressive production from a young lady whose ability as a proser will be further manifested later in the chapter:

Personification

I am hard to grasp. All over the world people regard me with reproachfulness and fear. Some try to cover me with wishful thinking. I am always victor in these cases. I enclose all emotions. No one can escape me, for I am reality.

—Mary Currier

Although the concept of integration does not necessarily apply to race mixture, nearly all of my students interpret it that way. Most of their ideas and solutions to the race problem reflect various degrees of immaturity, but often enough (making the assignment worthwhile) some clear-thinking youngster takes a rational approach to the subject and manages—even in the limited milieu of a single paragraph—the kind of astute observation one hardly expects from adults, as in the following:

Forced Integration

Recently, the Supreme Court handed down its decision on integration in Southern schools. Some Southern leaders are opposing their ruling. I think they're wrong in doing this, but I stand behind them 100% in their opposition to forced bussing. Certainly, the Southern schools are segregated, but so are many Northern schools. When Milwaukee was remodeling the Hawley Road School, many white children were to be bussed down to Erwin Mac Dowal School, a predominantly black institution. A rather large skirmish developed. Finally, Milwaukee won out, and whites were bussed into the ghetto area. This same thing is happening in Mississippi, and whites are building private schools just to keep their children away from Negroes. It is quite evident that the Supreme Court's methods are not going to work. It would help, I feel, if school districts were to be realigned, both in the North and in the South. Above all, if each side gives a little and tries to understand the other, integration could be as painless as putting on a sock or shoe. All it takes is a little sanity, and one of our major problems would be solved.

—Curt Weber

You don't have to agree with Curt's viewpoint, but you must applaud his attempt to inject a bit of simplicity into a situation which has admittedly become appallingly complex.

The Multi-Paragraph Composition

But you can't stay with the single-paragraph forever, as if your students would let you. Occasionally, they even beat you there. Some of them have been ready for the transition for quite some time, and in all likelihood were when they came to you.

It is at this point in your writing program that you discover new things about your charges. You find, for instance, that because of the additional latitude they have, their writing acquires more numerous evidences of that special literary trademark called style. Some even settle into a mood which characterizes their writing for a good share of the remaining school year. One student of mine, Mark Unak, whose haiku appears a bit further on in the chapter, wrote virtually every one of his compositions in Russian dialect, starring two or more of the following characters: Beshnov, Stalino, Zorrokovich, Sergeant Garciavich, and a cosmonaut named Spitnik LVII. You even occasionally discover a subtle humorist in your midst:

Fear

I have a common malady called acrophobia. This is fear of high places. I don't think that definition is absolutely correct as I don't get acrophobia in an airplane. In an airplane I get airsick.

I first noticed my fear while I was climbing Lapham Peak tower, near Delafield. Although I had great confidence in the fact that the tower was structurally secure, I was clutching the railing for dear life after 50 feet. Another 15 feet and I had finished a short prayer. After getting to the top, I sat firmly entrenched on a big wooden seat and looked at the view. I discovered that if one stared at the moving clouds on a windy day, he could actually imagine that the tower is tipping.

I can write this and laugh at myself now that I'm on the ground but if I were up there I would just be entering a coma now. After all, that tower is over 30 years old and it just could tip someday.

—*John Blazek*

The first thing you detect in a composition like this is the skill with which the young author moves from the general to the specific. The self-demeaning tone, cloaked in unspectacular statements of fact about his chicken-heartedness, reminds you of that technique so ably developed by the late great Robert Benchley.

From another student in the same class with John—produced on the same day—a grimmer view of the same subject:

It Is from Fear

Fear is a vicious giant stalking our lives and casting his horrid shadow upon us.

We are all motivated at least partly, by fear. It is because of the fear of being yelled at that we do things the "right way." It is because of our fear of failing that we study for tests. It is through fear of theft that we buy guns. It is because of the fear of riots that one of our largest cities bought a tank, an army tank, to use against our own people. It is fear that causes us to send men with fixed bayonets against our own children on the campuses of America.

It is from fear that hate comes. Blind, ignorant, clawing hate, for you can only hate what you don't know or understand. And it is fear that will not let us understand.

But there are men who don't fear. They are not afraid to show us our wrongs. But we fear them. We hate them. We laugh at them. We kill their bodies. But not their souls. You cannot kill a man who is not afraid of dying. His ideas, his soul remains.

Out of fear comes only trouble.

But out of intrepidness comes the change of the world.

Out of it comes hope.

—Pamela Marquardt

Perhaps you recall Pamela the poetess in Chapter 2. No slouch at prose either, this young writer. Yet, the above has a distinctly poetic flavor, doesn't it?

Still another creation from the same class on the same day:

Fear

Fear.

Close-up of a child in Viet Nam. The camera focuses on a teeming slum in Saigon. The child is a barefoot girl leading her little brother by the hand. A rocket slams into the dilapidated shack they call home . . .

Fear.

The camera zeroes in on a Biafran mother. She is holding a child in her arms. The child consists mainly of a bony skeleton, with a little skin stretched over his frame. The mother wonders, "Will my child be next to die?"

Fear.

The scene is a hotel corridor. A candidate reaches to shake the hand of a kitchen worker. Suddenly the corridor is turned into a hell of blood and tears and screams . . .

Fear.

Close-up of a Chicago street corner. A hippie yells, "The Whole World's watching." A club descends on his head . . .

Fear.

These pictures in rapid succession: bombs, a burning slum, guns, a burning flag . . .

Fear.

—Lisa Martin

Remember Lisa in Chapter 2, who seldom missed an opportunity for commentary on the human condition?

For a bit of whimsy, now, see what you think of this one:

Writing Poetry

I enjoy reading poetry far more than writing it. In fact, I even like writing paragraphs more than writing poetry. I shall never be a great poet, nor, unfortunately, do I have any great urge to be. Writing poetry to me is a kind of semi-conscious affair. I believe that to write some of the things I do with full consciousness would be too much of a shock for me.

Seriously now, when I begin to write poetry, I sit down and calmly wait for an inspiration. That is, with a sudden surge of brain power, I manage to form an idea, with which I shall start my great piece: "The Cat."

After I have successfully written the first line, I must make some great decisions. First, I must decide what kind of pattern my poem will have. There are infinite varieties of patterns, but since this poem will have only one stanza, there won't be much difference no matter what I do. The other question is whether or not this poem will rhyme. It must have a beat, but need not rhyme. Since "cat" will be fairly easy to rhyme, let's see if we can make a rhyming poem.

        The cat
        That—
            Ate the rat
            Got fat.

Very good, now—on to the finish!

There are two definite qualities an ending phrase can have. It
can either be a surprise ending, giving the poem a "bang," or a
finishing phrase, concluding a thought started someplace else. This
ending demonstrates the latter:

        The cat
        That—
            Ate the rat
            Got fat.
                Poor rat-filled fat cat.

                                        —*Kathy Lorinczi*

Here is an adolescent who has acquired the knack of lending
sophistication to the trifling. The pedantic air is precisely what
gives the above essay its charm. Would you call it studied humor?

The class from which this came was given in this assignment
full latitude with the area of subject matter, the human activity
of communicating.

You find sentimentalists by the dozens in the ranks of adolescents. Behold the work of one:

Just Another Concert

The guitars stand alone on the stage. Three singers run out.
Cameras flash as newsmen and fans take pictures. The spotlight
focuses, and to us in the audience it seems an eternity before the
singing starts.

Finally, the songs come and they are worth waiting for. As folk
songs do, they tell of love and hate, peace and war. The minutes
fly and the singers leave the stage. We applaud wildly, hoping for
a few encores, and they are sung. Half an hour passes and the
guitars again stand alone and silent on the stage. We ask for autographs, and they are given.

Everything is over now; audience and singers go their separate
ways. For us the singing should never have ended, because this was

one of the few folk concerts we shall ever see. For them it was just another performance.

—*Jane Currier*

What better way to tell your reader how much an experience has meant to you than with the technique this young authoress uses in contrasting her two final ideas. The essay is a study in crescendo—from lone guitars to camera flashes, spotlights, action, applause, the excitement of given autographs, and back again to lone guitars, the silent stage. All of it done in soft pastels.

This assignment was one of the human activity series in our writing program. Again, it's "communicating."

Jane's older sister Mary, whom it was also my good fortune to teach, wrote with the same kind of sensitivity to the world around her. In the years that she and Jane passed through my class, the two had recently moved here from the East, and Mary used to talk with me by the hour about her first love, the Maryland bay country. I never really understood how strong the attachment was until one day in late fall when she turned in a composition titled "The Last Walk":

As I started for the upper beach today I had a lump in my throat, for this would be my last walk on the shore. There was a swift breeze from the river and the sand was still cool in the early morning. The tide was coming in. Its lapping noises, blended with the wind in my ears, gave me a feeling of oneness with the beach, river, and sky.

I thought back to the other times when I had marveled at the river. In the fall the mornings echoed with the sounds of birds. Then the river was loaded with all kinds of fowl, diving now and then for fish and clams. For hours at a time I would sit gazing out at the waves and swans.

Before the birds arrived I would be down on the seawall. In the evening I found a comfortable spot on the sand where I could watch the sun set in a grand climax of reds, oranges, and pinks. While a strong wind tossed the reeds and willows, the moon shone and the stars peeped out from behind the dark misty clouds. The waves breaking on the sand, the wind in the grass and trees, and the mysterious sky, all seemed to combine in an atmosphere of tranquillity.

Now the river was sparkling with sun and deep blues and greens twinkling off shore. I turned and looked up at the bank to acknowledge the massive loblolly pine which held it together. The pine's cones were scattered about the lawn. Some were even down in the tidal pool at my feet where a few dead jelly fish shared quarters with seaweed and minnows.

For a while I lingered by a patch of seaweed to observe a game of tag between two sand fleas. Then, looking up at the sun, I realized the time. I would have to hurry in order to finish my walk before noon, when I would leave my home by the river.

Reluctantly I struck out for a reed-covered part of the beach where there had once been two ponds. Upon reaching it I found not only an overgrowth of weeds, but also all sorts of trash that people had thoughtlessly dumped there. Where there had once been ponds surrounded by grass and flowers with insects buzzing and a few crabs, there were now old tires, tin cans, broken glass, and even tiles from someone's floor.

Farther up the beach I encountered huge logs imbedded in the sand, crawling with insects and vines. They were coated with slime and eroding badly. On the sand lay countless pebbles, bits of shells, sharks' teeth, bones, and dead fish.

Here the forest met the river. Fallen trees lay with leaves in the water and soaked roots in the soil. Huge clay pits took the place of banks while piles of gnarled vines, large stones, and rotten trees were the only seawall. On top of the clay-pits wild roses and honeysuckle rambled in fields of wild wheat and clover.

The forest, river, and beach were filled with nature's beauty this morning. I wished that this could be like any other day and that I wasn't really leaving—that it was all a bad dream. But I *was* leaving and I couldn't afford to be late. No matter how hard I hoped or prayed, it would be useless.

With one last look at the end of the beach and forest, I turned around and walked home.

—*Mary Currier*

I would have to say that "The Last Walk" is the best piece of descriptive narrative I ever got from a student.

As an English teacher, you just have to have special affection for the student who writes the kind of exposition you are about to read. The assignment called for a multi-paragraph composition. Subject matter once more the human activity of communicating:

How to Do Writing Assignments

To many students, writing and creative writing assignments are real torture. Whether we like it or not, though, writing assignments are here to stay. We might as well learn to write well and enjoy writing.

The first step in writing is to choose a subject. Usually the assignment limits your choice. A subject that you know or have had experience with is best. If you must write on a topic you know little about, study it. The library has material on almost everything. Spend some time thinking about your topic. What do you want to say, how are you going to say it? Have a general outline in mind, then put in detail. Copy what you have neatly so you can put in more corrections and still have your paper legible. Check for errors in spelling and punctuation. Scan the paper for errors in grammar and sentence structure. Have you said exactly what you set out to? When you are satisfied with your work, copy it over neatly to hand in.

—Wendy Carson

Besides being lovable, the authoress obviously possesses considerable organizational talent. And she practiced what she preached. Here's another one of Wendy's which demonstrates the tone she reflected most frequently in her writing:

A Solution

America doesn't seem to want to come to a showdown with the Soviet Union on their overdue bill at the U. N., fearful that they might find other ways of controlling world affairs besides with the vote.

A compromise in punishment might be enough of an annoyance to delegates to force Russia to pay up, while avoiding punishments great enough to justify their "getting even." Why not make the Russian delegates go to the end of the cafeteria line? That would make them unpopular to eat with and would hurt their image. Or they could be banned from the delegates' bar. We could take their parking spaces away. They'd find it hard to explain that they bombed us because they got fed up with walking to the assembly all the way from where they were parked in Yonkers.

In ways like these we can force the Soviet Union to pay up their U. N. tab without the showdown the U. S. is so desperately avoiding.

There is something disarming about an eighth grader who keeps abreast of what's happening in international politics. This, of course, was written at the time when a previously unpublicized fact came to light in the nation's press. The composition came on a day when students were allowed to choose their own subject matter. This kind of latitude, incidentally, not infrequently results in exceptionally entertaining creations by young writers.

Two more such "subject-matter-of-your-choice" creations follow:

Remembering

I seem to have a talent for remembering all sorts of stupid things. Sometimes at dinner, when the conversation is getting dull, I tell about some sleep survey which showed that most women sleep on their stomachs and most men sleep on their backs. Or a new powder invented for catching criminals: Just add water and you get a surface 100 times more slippery than ice. Now what use is there in knowing a thing like that? Unless you are a criminal. My mother calls me a "fund of useless information."

I guess I memorize music easily. If I can play a piece with the book, I can play it without the book. My mother thinks it's wonderful to memorize easily, but I really don't see what the advantage is as long as I have the book anyway. Do you?

I remember things about horses too. If I have had time to read a horse book carefully, I can remember it almost word for word. At night when I can't get to sleep I "read" the book again in my mind: "The thoroughbred originated in England when fiery little desert stallions were crossed with the native mares. The result was a horse so swift that today he can outrun even the fleetest Arab." And so on.

And of course, like a lot of people, I remember a lot about kindergarten and grade school. Sometimes my family gets mad at me because I am always remembering.

The only kind of stuff I can't remember is schoolwork or anything else important. This may sound silly, but it's true. I'll study for hours for a test and not remember a thing. Everybody tells me to try harder, but I do! Do you think I like getting low grades? So I have a theory. I must just remember what I like to remember. All my information seems interesting to *me*. All the piano pieces I like I really memorize quickly. Of course, I love horses so I'd really remember almost anything about them, and as for remembering old times, I only remember pleasant old times.

I must be either narrow-minded or crazy.

—*Laura Miesbauer*

Laura's grades—I recall—were not all that low. And I'm certain she was not aware of just how bright she was. Humor in writing delights me, which is one reason why I always looked forward to her next composition. She seldom disappointed me.

Years ago, the composition you are about to read would have taken no one by surprise. But today . . .

America

America has been praised in poetry, prose, and song. It has been written about by people of all races, of all religions, and of all creeds. It has been glorified and it has been criticized by so many people in so many different ways simply because it is America.

Motherhood is the heart of America. It is large and comforting. It provides strength and protection. It is generous and tender as it maintains unity among the sister states. It can fight when necessary and defend when attacked. It can feed and supply and meet every demand. It can create warmth in relations with neighboring countries and distant lands.

Rights as they are granted in the constitution are the arteries of America. They make life worth living. They give the privilege of writing, speaking, and assembling freely. They permit worship, guarantee privacy, and provide protection. They make up the circulation and provide the necessary nourishment.

Ideals are the eyes of America. They are many and they are set high, but they can be reached. They are a goal worth attaining, because they have been set by years of struggle and strife. They have been set by the brave, the restless, and the hopeful. The aim is high, but progress lies in this direction.

America is a living thing. It is ever growing and always moving in all directions. It has a heartbeat and a brain. It has joy and laughter, sorrow and tears. It has fears and pain, pride and prejudice. It has feet and it moves quickly, but never too fast to take on another passenger. It is America.

—*Daphne Panagis*

If you had asked for metaphoric consistency and a final paragraph of succinct summing up in a student composition, you could hardly be happier. The authoress was just as soulful as her prose—tiny, with dark complexion, large deep brown eyes, and sparkling smile—all of which were practically incidental to her prowess as a writer.

Once upon a time when our writing unit was more autobiographically oriented than in more recent years, one title that consistently elicited entertaining composition from my students was "My Secret Ambition." What you are about to read is another of those pristinely simple premises developed as only adolescents can develop them:

My Secret Ambition

Ever since I started playing the French horn, I have dreamed of the perfect horn. I have imagined this horn as a shining, flawless instrument, perfect in every detail. It would be very different from the scratched and dented horn that I am renting from the school. I have always thought of my dream horn as the best ever made and a delight to play.

Since it is rather difficult to find a French horn of this quality in a junior high school band, it was hard for me to actually picture this horn. My first look at just such a horn was at my private lesson. As my teacher opened his case and carefully took out his horn, I immediately recognized it as my dream horn. Yes, this was the kind of horn I wanted to own some day.

Of course now the problem is when. Since a French horn in such perfect condition is quite expensive, I think of the day that I will own my own horn as being in the distant future. But then, who knows? Just last Saturday I took a step in the right direction. I bought my own mouthpiece.

—Mary Brauer

There is in those three paragraphs as much about Mary Brauer as her dream horn—all of it between the lines. I think Mary is at the university now, and I often wonder if she ever got the shiny brass to go with that mouthpiece.

The Narrative with Dialogue

A school year never ends that I don't marvel at what students can do with this literary genre, given the time and the opportunity. Here is where the now generation takes every opportunity to throw its unique dialect at us adults, as witness the following, the product of instructions to write a dialogue involving three or more people:

The Discussion

"Coolness!" a wide-eyed saddle-shoe fanatic shouted.

"Aak, phooey!" someone said. "Snicker, snicker," he added.

"Wearing saddle-shoes makes me insanely happy!" I said to my ditto-shoed friend.

"Yeah, us people whose triumphant pursuit of happiness is unparalleled in saddle-shoes."

"Where did you dig up that one?" I questioned.

No answer. We continued down the hall exchanging hi's and receiving strange glares.

"Two pair of Howard shoes in one day," Mr. Mathie sighed. "A-a-ugh!" he slid in before we were out of hearing range.

"By a bizarre twist of fate, I bet half the—"

"Oh ha ha ha hee hee!" interrupted someone.

She started again. "By a bizarre twist of fate, I bet half the kids will have them in a couple of weeks."

I felt the need for a quiet, "I hope."

The whappity-whappity-whap of the thick rubber soles announced our entrance into class.

"How terribly hideous!" one girl cried.

"A-choo!" a boy exploded. "Germs! Disease! Infection!" he continued, pretending pain. "I think I'm allergic to saddle-shoes!"

"Zow!" cried another boy, "do they glow in the dark?"

After class I parted with my saddle-shoed friend. I was accompanied by another friend now, getting his opinion all the way to our next class. "You nitwit! You birdbrain! Why? Why! They're uncool, you blockhead! Blah! Complete blah-dom!" he continued. "Sigh! Know something? I like them."

Confused and baffled, my saddle-shoes and I still whump on.

—Jennifer Golz

Narrative-with-dialogue lends itself rather well also to the budding and rare young science-fictioner:

2136 A. D.

"Vorr," crackled the voice on the intercom, waking me up. "Time for school."

"Right, mom," I replied as I slipped a pair of earphones over my head, plugged them into a control panel on the wall of my room, and slumped into a chair in front of the eduscreen.

"All right, now, hand in your homework," the instructor said. I reached over my desk, took card K32A and fed it into a slot on the eduscreen set. The instructor explained how to find remote vanutalvity using a Richencoff meter—and other equally boring subjects. An hour later I turned off the screen and went downstairs for meal one.

After three nutrient tablets and a good old-fashioned just-like-1967 pancake, I went out and had a game of leviball with seven of my friends. Unfortunately, we lost, 7 to 12. We were just about to start another game when the universal siren blew and we had to go back to our houses via the moving sidewalks.

—Dave Zentner

Obviously the narrative is plotless, but nonetheless effective and entertaining. And it is simply because the young author never over-reaches himself. He knows the limits he must observe when writing this kind of thing, and he observes them, the result being complete credibility. The young man in question had a puckish face along with that creative bent.

What's the best thing to do with "characters" who pass under your tutelage? Let them write. The young authoress whom you are about to read was, besides a unique human being, acutely aware of human foibles. Her bizarre sense of humor and effusive smile could brighten any classroom. Her writing reflects her character:

Forgotten Friend

"Hi, Andy!" shouted a plump little girl around nine years of age, as she pelted down the walk. "What do you want to do?"

"I don't know, Gail."

"Want to play circus?"

"Nah."

"How about 'army'?"

"Nah. Let's play Davy Crockett."

"That isn't any fun with just two people."

"Well, let's go get Mark then."

"Okay, beat you to the door."

Dashing up to the door they stopped on the porch and panted

heavily for awhile before ringing the bell. Mark appeared quickly and after the usual salutations said, "Well, what do you guys want to do?"

"Let's play Davy Crockett!" exclaimed Andy.

"Okay," he agreed. "Gonna go down by the river?"

"Sure," Gail said. "Let's go."

"I'm going to be Davy," Mark stated loudly.

"You are not! I'm going to be Davy!" shouted Gail.

"I'm going to be an Indian," Andy said, taking careful aim at a street light and hitting it with a large stone.

"Guess I will be too," Gail added.

By this time they had reached the entrance to the woods, a steep path leading down to what the kids called Alligator Pits. Soon they came to a smaller path. Andy and Gail sat on a log by the river. "Mark," said Gail, "you go and hide in the woods. We will count to 300 and then track you down."

"Right," said Mark, and turning quickly he disappeared down the path.

"Gail?"

"Yeah, Andy?"

"Let's go home. This isn't any fun."

"Okay. We'll go to my house and get something to eat."

—*Gail Sauter*

Another example of the three-or-more-persons dialogue narrative. In this kind of writing you hope for a natural tone to the conversation, reasonably accurate punctuation, and at least some description—so the mischievous ending is a bonus. The technique, though quite rare among young writers, appears at pleasantly spaced intervals. The specific assignment, in case you were wondering, that generated "Forgotten Friend" was another in the human activities area, namely, "play."

Poetry

There is poetry in youth. Even their movements are poetic. Watch the before-classes morning promenade in the corridors, the basketball and football squads in action, or the young co-ed cheerleaders—first or second string. The problem is to capture some of it on paper in your English classroom. It is a struggle well worth the rewards:

A Delicious Kingdom

The sun is a big fresh grapefruit.
Its rays are bright sweet juice.
The stars were formed by tiny drops
That somehow jiggled loose.

The moon is a black-eyed sweet pea
That looks at the earth at night.
The earth is a jolly fat grape
That squirts out seeds in flight.

—Kathryn Schutz

The above is not the result of a poetry assignment, per se. It was composed during the week that we developed the concept of the universe, and I gave the class "full latitude," which meant they could go into poetry-writing if they wished. The rhyme pattern evident here—a b c b with trimeter beat, is not a bad form to begin with when you are teaching poetry to junior and senior high school students. You have probably discovered as I have that this pattern is manifested in student poetry-writing as often as any other—I suppose because of its simplicity. Somehow, while reading this, I got the feeling that during our survey Kathy must have been paying very close attention when we talked about the poet and metaphor. The original analogy in the second stanza immediately brings to mind our frequent space probes. I wish I had said it.

Kathy, incidentally, used to come up with the roughest rough drafts in her class. I never attempted to intercede at that stage of her writing, mainly because so much of it was indecipherable. She would scritch and scratch until I was sure she was never going to arrive at anything substantive or even legible, but by the middle of the second day, I would find her busily transcribing her scribblings into what always turned out to be some of the best prose and poetry ever written by my students over the years.

You can expect humor in adolescents' poetry as well as in their prose. The following poem has an interesting form, don't you think? How to describe it: Almost couplet with a random meter? Clearly, it's the content, though, that gives it its appeal:

In That Folder

From the cradle to the hearse,
My whole darn life fits into one little verse.
I live, but I don't move.
And I carry my brain in a folder marked "German II."
I'm a morbid kid,
I remember everything I ever did.
If five months ago you were to ask me
Just what it was I planned to be,
I would have told you, rather happily,
"I plan to teach."
But now, I find that even that, is beyond my reach.
I'm a morbid kid, y'know,
And most say I'll never grow.
I live, but I don't move,
And I carry my brain in a folder marked "German II."

—Victoria Cazel

Much of what Vicki wrote was "self-demeaning" in this same brightly humorous way. From her performance as an English student, notwithstanding the poetic comment, I'd have to say that some day she will be eminently qualified to teach, if she only wants to.

The human activity of fighting spawned this very feminine approach to the subject in tetrameter verse, with lines 9 and 10 effectively unstrapping an otherwise hidebound metrical pattern:

Who Cares?

I sat on the grass under a tree,
Watching two boys fighting for me.
Tom smashed George right in the nose,
And I calmly watched, smelling a rose.
George got mad and swore out loud—
I gazed at the sky watching a cloud.
These mad boys were a blur to my eyes,
As I whistled a tune and swatted at flies.
All this silly fighting (oh what a sight),

Just to settle who will take me out tonight.
Gee, what a shock the winner will get
When I tell him I have to baby-sit.

—*Kristi Knuijt*

Kristi was a punchline artist—even as a proser. She was also our champion orator, possessing a booming voice completely belying her appearance. She had a thirst for learning such as I have scarcely seen in an adolescent, and if progress can be detected in one student among 150, it was certainly apparent in Kristi during the ten months she wrote for me.

Winter's Death

As I watch
Jack Frost silently etch
a frozen masterpiece
on my windowpane,
snowflakes tumble down
from a mournful sky.

Frightened bare trees shudder
as the cold North wind
breathes Death
upon a quiet planet.

The snow-blanket covers
the sleeping land,
and the countryside waits
to be reborn
in spring.

—*Lucy Hille*

An interesting study in free verse by a young lady who was just as quietly majestic as her poetry. Not many adolescents are willing or able to try their luck with this kind of unfettered expression, but look further at the work on the next page, composed by that rare breed of student whom you recall simply because you witnessed her gradually overcome her writing problems to become one of your best:

Alone with the Dawn

The dawn has arrived,
Finally. I've been waiting
To stroll along the shore
Watching seagulls soar upward.
I'm going to meet the horizon—
Oh, no, I've never met it.
Maybe today.

The sand will feel cool between my toes;
The salt air will blow past my cheeks;
The water will come up lapping the shore—
Then it will fall back into the sea.

The morning brings freshness,
I'm going to enjoy it.
Soon it will be covered with the fog of human misery and hate.
Hurry! Come with me before it's too late.

                                        —*Patti Grove*

Particularly impressive is the repetitive modal reinforcement in Patti's second stanza, and of course the lovely metaphor in the final stanza.

I daresay if this next creation were to be put to music, it would have to have a Wagnerian timbre to it:

Forest Fire

The forest fire is a woman.
She has many bright fingers.
They flicker through the black tree-bars of her prison.
She is going to die in the morning.

  Push, pull, strain, beat!
  Rage at your black prison bars!
  The rising of dawn will seal your doom;
  Now watch the setting stars.

She reaches far, she reaches high.
The morning comes too fast.
She is a great beauty,
Why should she not last?

Push, pull, strain, beat!
Flicker your fingers to the sky!
The dawn is sealing your few last hopes;
What is it like to die?

Already she hears her jailer's tread.
It is a wind which moves her to more straining.
She's got to escape or she will be dead,
But the executioner is coming.
She feels him!

Push, pull, strain, beat!
Now you must do your best!
If, at last, you cannot escape,
Then—you will be at rest.

The gray executioner drips on her.
The rain pulses in sheets on her.
As she dies her beauty dies with her.
All that is left is her last murmur.

Push, pull, strain, beat!
Could you not live more?
The death-rain came in a cold, gray sheet,
When the dawn shut your life's door.

She has left only the black, bare bars of her prison.
There is only the executioner rain pouring down in cloaks of death.
The forest fire was a beautiful woman.
She died this morning.

—*Pamela Peterson*

I suppose the idea of a forest fire being a woman is what is so
fascinating about this unusual blend of description and narrative. It is almost pure imagery. Its theme and mood, the recur-
ring mournful refrain, are somewhat reminiscent of Poe. The
pattern is chaotic, the refrain itself even moving randomly between trimeter and tetramater. But I think it is the pattern ir-
regularity which gives the poem its effect—somehow capturing
the ambivalent mood of the beautiful lady.

A dark-eyed, raven-haired young lady by the name of Sue

Rothman composed the next poem, which looks at the problems of adolescents through mock-serious eyes and for the most part, trimeter verse:

A Teenager's Lament

The world is a difficult place to live—
Decisions everywhere;
What to eat, where to go,
And what on earth to wear.

    Should I choose the blue dress,
    Or will it be the brown?
    Should I see a movie,
    Or get my shopping done downtown?

Should I eat that piece of cake,
Or should I eat the pie?
Should I wear my hair down low,
Or comb it up quite high?

    Should I play the radio,
    Or the phonograph?
    Will the TV show I watch
    Make me cry or laugh?

Does my boy friend really care?
Will he be true blue?
Will he always just be mine,
Or find somebody new?

    It's difficult to be my age
    And with these problems strive,
    But with a little effort,
    I shall probably survive.

How's the following for a bit of Ogden Nash in tetrameter from the distaff side:

The Pencil

The pencil is a handy thing,
The length is always varying;
It's found in almost every shade,
Some even come with your name engraved.

A pen is fine for many things
Like writing words for sing-along-sings.
But for math and French, et cetera,
Give me a pencil, it's really much bettera.

—*Lynn Scherer*

And this from our humorous friend, Vicki Cazel, once again:

School's Out

A trail of crumbs, an apple core,
The Journal Green Sheet on the floor,
A pile of books, a half shut door,
I know my brother's home once more!

Snowy boots dropped in the hall,
Two boys downstairs playing ball,
The radio turned to a muted roar,
I know my brother's home once more!

In all likelihood you are aware that the young male adolescent is nowhere near as prolific at poetry-writing as his female counterpart, which fact I think can perhaps be partly explained by the difference in maturity between the two. Here, however, are a few lyrical stanzas and one very good exercise in free verse—decidedly masculine in tone and subject—by male poets, followed by haiku from both sexes, which oddly enough, boys produce quite readily:

A Drift or Three

When I see it start to snow,
My aches and pains begin to grow.
For I can see a drift or three,
In the drive at the house next door to me.

For you see I've made a pact,
To keep it clean both front and back
And when I see that drift or three,
It means a lot of work for me.

—*Scott Ferguson*

The Fireman

He is on the watch tonight;
Ready to work, set to fight.

Cool he is,
Coward he's not.
This is the fireman,
Best of the lot.

He is captain of a squad,
For his age this is odd.

Many a fire
He does tame.
This is the fireman,
Remember his name.

From fires he's fought—you can tell
He knows his job and does it well.

He risks his life
In crackling flame.
The silent hero,
Without any fame.

—Bob Mueller

Both of these poems were the result of specific poetry assignments which we borrowed from the human activity segment of our writing unit. "Work" was the catalyst.

In an earlier chapter, I mentioned that free-verse writing among adolescents belonged almost exclusively in the feminine domain. That is not to say the male adolescent doesn't occasionally invade successfully. Recently, a bright young man in one of my morning classes waxed Sandburgian on me during a specific poetry-writing caper in which we again borrowed from the human activities segment of our unit—"sleep" to be exact:

Dreams

Dreams are a fourth dimension:
You can go shoot elephants
In deep dark Africa
Or get run over by a train.
Dreams can take you anywhere—
Into Westminster Abbey
Or down to the ocean floor.
You can go in a rocket ship

Out to the planet Mars
Or climb the highest peak
In all the world.
You could be
A great football hero
Or a drunken bum
Lying in the street.
You could save the world
By catching the giant martian bomb
Or be a street-sweeper in Cincinnati.
You could explore the polar ice,
Or strike oil in Arabia
With twenty wives and fifty servants,
All yours.
You might direct a Broadway hit
Or go broke in the process:
A nightmare.
If you can dream
You can go anywhere—
Anywhere in the world
And beyond.

                              —*Gordon Hering*

Quite a litany of contrasts, isn't it? Who dreams better with his
eyes open than a teenager?

You recall, I hope, our discussion earlier of the Japanese art
form haiku. What follow are recent products of nine of my
classes. Genuine haiku, as we mentioned, deals with nature, but
you will see that we bend a little in this respect. The art form as
a vehicle for self-expression lends itself admirably to a wide
variety of voices, which with the application of a little adolescent
ingenuity, can be made compatible with the great voice of nature. There is, for example, the voice of quiet outrage over our
befouled environment:

                Air is fresh and clean
                with no worry in the world
                until man is born.

                              —*Hans Mueller*

Lakes with blue water
Clean, clear, beautiful water
Are seldom seen now.

—*Craig Weiss*

The voice of plaintive commentary:

Beautiful morning,
Blue sky, fresh air, cooling breeze,
But I go to school.

—*Tony Steiner*

Bird high in the sky
Sings a song of joy to us
Does not get one back.

—*Mark Irgens*

Running brooks and streams,
Fish, many, easy to catch—
Me alone with none.

—*Cindy Savage*

The voice of simple observation:

Gloomy overcasts,
Rainswept streets and thunderheads.
Once again it's spring.

—*David Chopp*

Jewels from rooftops,
Transparent gems in the sun,
Tapered icicles.

—*Sarah Ream*

Hundreds of years old
Spruce trees stand in the forest
Towering over us.

—*Jim Schreiber*

Die Sterne, spielen
Fast allein in dem Himmel,
So still, wie die Nacht.

—*Kathy Plehn*

Reddest is the rose
that grows so wild and so free
yet so tenderly.

—*Toni Roehl*

At one end a swamp
At the other an island
Between's deep water.

—*Carl Stenholm*

Peacock, pet of queens
Flashing tail of green-gold eyes
Waving in the breeze.

—*Barbara Bruns*

Green and charcoal brown
Valleys low and mountains high
Sloping and jagged.

—*Judi Gaulke*

The buoyant voice:

Bears are gay at play
It's honey they like so well
Their paws serve as spoons.

—*Mark Naegel*

Nature is funny
Every time she does her thing,
It's never the same.

—*David Reiss*

The voice of candor:

My eighth hour class
Is just like a tornado—
All it is is wind.

—*David Rudig*

The voice that personifies:

The sun sets quickly
To let the moon have its turn
At watching the world.

—*Roy Setum*

Pink fingers moving
Gently through silver softness
The world sighs, dawn comes.

—Jenny Rearick

Compassionate cloud,
Pauses to weep as he sees
Man's unhappiness.

—Lisa Martin

The facetious voice:

See Smokey the Bear
A fire has singed his hair.
Don't play with matches.

—Cheri Henke

The ants are coming—
They will be all around us!
They are eating Fred!!

—Mark Unak

The voice of the philosopher:

Life, death, and progress
Cures of disease; love and hate
All products of time.

—Jim Kronwall

On seeing your nest
I take your egg in my palm
Wanting my own wings.

—Sue Hargis

Silver moon rises
Blemished by a shadow of
Man the trespasser.

—Linda Fibich

Of the romantic:

The day becomes night.
With a flashlight, wood is found,
And placed in a pile.

Add a match. And then
A wonderful thing happens.
Color fills the dark.

Reds, oranges, whites
Tongues of flame devour the dark.
Stars and fire. Love.

—Kurt Hanson

And the voice of deep affection:

What is a mother?
Part of me, her flesh and blood
A woman of love.

—Regina Thomas

The young communicators who wrote all of the selections you have just read are gone now.

Some are in high school; some are halfway through college; some are hard at work making a living for themselves.

But they left me something to remember them by—mementoes of paths that met and parted again.

Because they put themselves on record often, we knew each other just that much more intimately; and just as important, because of it they are still around.

I keep them in an old canvas-topped binder in a corner of my office where every June they are joined by others.

Some understood better than their colleagues what was expected of them, but all of them took the task in hand with whatever ingenuity and industry they were capable of.

Together we pursued, I think, enough variety so that the vast majority found their niche—or at least felt they did.

And that is terribly important—to them and to you.

On life's mad turnpike
seek solace at the wayside
of self-fulfillment.

INDEX

A

Addition, 158
Addition, revision, 69, 70
Aims in language course, 18
Alliteration, 64, 151, 152
American Poets 1800–1900, 156
Anapestic foot, 154
Assignments, sequential, 22
Attitudes, 25–26
Attributal break, 56
Attributive, 54, 55, 56, 57
Audience contact, 80, 96

B

Book reports, oral, 80–81, 98
Busywork, 36

C

Cassette tape recorder, 98–99
Cavalcade of Poems, 151, 153
Classes oversized:
    alleviating pain, 29–33
    depersonalize education, 19
    oral presentation, 20
    reason for neglect, 23
Classes oversized *(contd.)*
    work load, 20
    written composition, 20
College, 26
Comma value, 54, 55, 56
Comments, written, 74
Committees, 18, 24–25
Communication:
    active, 19, 22
    passive, 22
Composition, 41–45, 78–101, 181–190, 190–199
    (see also Oral composition)
Conjunctionitis, 91–92
Content, oral composition, 89
Continuity, 46
Contradiction, 158
Conventional attributive, 54, 55, 56
Correcting, inter-student, 132–133
Creativity, 180–215
    (see also Productivity, creative)
Currents in Poetry, 151
Curriculum guides:
    active communication, 19, 22
    aims in language course, 18
    clear, concise communications, 18

219

developmental sequence, 19
Curriculum guides (*contd.*)
  enumerated goals, 22
  exercises, 22
  frequency of teaching composition,
    18, 19
  grammar, 105
  language analysis, 22
  language used, 18
  literature, 23
  little time for composition, 22
  presumptions, 19
  sequence and scope, 18, 23
  sequential assignments, 22
  subject matter, 23
  texts to be used, 23
  transcending, 27–29
  vocabulary, 23

D

Dactyllic foot, 154
"David," 156
Debureaucratize, 34–35
Delivery, oral composition, 89
Depersonalization in education, 20
Description, 45–46, 47
Designs in Poetry, 153
Developmental reading, 141–142
  (*see also* Reading lab)
Developmental sequence, 19
Dialogue, 54–58, 199–202
  (*see also* Writing)
Diction, 46, 94–95
Dictionary, 120
Discontinuity, oral composition, 94
Discussion, student-oriented, 81–83
  (*see also* Oral composition)
Ditto-ness, 157
Drillwork:
  grammar, 20, 35–36
  vocabulary, 133–134

E

Elimination, revision, 68, 70
Enunciation, oral composition, 95
Evaluation, student:
  constructive criticism, 170–171
  entertainment, 175–178

Evaluation, student (*contd.*)
  negative comments, 172–173
  positivism, 173–174
  pragmatic view, 169–170
  suggested alternatives, 174–175
  summary, 178–179
Evaluations:
  grammar, 112, 117
  oral composition, 88–89, 99–100
  vocabulary, 134–135
Evangeline, 150–152
Exams (*see* Tests)
Exclamation mark, 55
Exercises, 22
Exposition, 46–47
Expression, oral composition, 93

F

Folders, 75
Free verse, 65

G

Goals, enumerated, 22
Grades, 21, 23, 37–38
Graduate work, 18
Grammar:
  analysis of student writing, 110–113
    adjective and verbal clusters, 112
    class discussion, 111
    demonstration, 111–112
    drillwork correction eliminated,
      113
    "grammarize" cumulatively, 112
    identifying labels not mandatory,
      111
    pages of student paragraphs, 110–
      111
    sentence drill eliminated, 112–113
    "short burst" method, 112
    year-end course evaluations, 112
  curriculum guide, 105
  drillwork, 20, 23
  few problems in student writing,
    116
  history of English, 106
  outline, 106–109
    before implementation, 110
    consolidation, 110

Grammar (contd.)
  outline (contd.)
    initial instruction phase, 110
    modifiers, 108–109
    nominal clause, 109
    nominal functions, 107–108
    page one, 106–107
    page three, 108–109
    page two, 107–108
    sentence-relatedness, 110
    three- or four-page, 106
    transformational generative ap-
      proach, 109–110
    verb, 106–107
    verb parts, 107
    verb tenses, 107
    verbals, 107
  reason for kind of program, 117
  re-evaluation, 117
  substitute for text, 105–110
  summary, 117–118
  techniques, 103–104
    fifteen minutes a week, 104
    following outline, 104
    minor stress, 103
    no written drill, 103
    sentences in context, 104
    ten hours a school year, 104
  testing, 113–116
    correct in 10 minutes, 113
    covers cumulative material, 113
    end of page of paragraphs, 113
    end of year, 113
    example, test number one, 113–
      114
    follow outline pages, 113
    grammar and composition, 115–
      116
    learning experience, 113–115
    multiple-choice statements, 113
    programed learning method,
      113
    reflects instructional program, 113
    three specific times, 113
  texts, 104–105
    approaches and terminology, 105
    create and compound confusion,
      105

Grammar (contd.)
  texts (contd.)
    stultifying experience, 104
    word position, 106
Groups, 20–21
Guide (see Curriculum guides)

H

Haiku, 66–68, 211–215
  (see also Productivity, creative)

I

Iambic foot, 153–154
Indenting, dialogue, 54, 57
Inferred attributive, 54, 55
Institutes, summer, 18

J

Jotting down ideas, 48

L

Language analysis, 22
Language in curriculum guide, 18
Leadership, oral composition, 78–79
Library, class, 138–139
Literature, 23, 120, 123

M

Markings, 74–75
Meetings, 25
Metaphor, 151, 152, 156
Meter, 153–154
  (see also Poetry)
Motivation, 180–215
  (see also Productivity, creative)

N

Narrative with dialogue, 199–202
Notes, dependency, 97–98
Noun of address, 56
Novel, 158–164
  (see also Reading lab)

O

Oblivia, 22
Oral composition:
  audience contact, 96
  class discussions, 79

Oral composition (*contd.*)
  conjunctionitis, 91–92
  content, 89
  delivery, 89
  dependency on notes, 97–98
  diction, 94–95
  discontinuity, 94
  effective communicator, 79
  enunciation, 95
  evaluation, 88–89
  experiences before audience, 80
  expression, 93
  formal presentations, 79–80
  importance, 78
  leadership, 78–79
  making an evaluation, 99–100
  need, 79
  neglect, 78
  oral book report, 80–81, 98
  playback, 98–99
  posture, 89–90
  resource unit, 84–88
  resulting young adult, 100
  self-confidence and poise, 80
  signalling, 97
  speed talker, 92–93
  student-oriented discussion, 81–83
    class temperament, 83
    effectiveness of delivery, 83
    every student, 81–82
    idea exchange, 82
    immature, 82
    number of presentations, 83
    observing students' reactions, 83
    one person at time, 82
    out of hand, 82
    teacher as listener, 81
    time limit, 83
    varying degrees, 82–83
  summary, 101
  television, 79
  too little or too much, 98
  volume, 95–96
Oral presentation, 20, 23
  (*see also* Oral composition)
Outline, grammar, 106–109
  (*see also* Grammar)

Oversized classes, 19-20, 23, 29–31
  (*see also* Classes, oversized)

P

Paperbacks, 137–140
  (*see also* Reading lab)
Paragraph, 45–46, 48, 49, 50–53, 58–59
Period value, 55, 56
Persuasion, 46, 47
Poems to Enjoy, 153
Poetry:
  addition, 158
  alliteration, 151, 152
  American Poets 1800–1900, 156
  Cavalcade of Poems, 151, 153
  contradiction, 158
  Currents in Poetry, 151
  "David," 156
  Designs in Poetry, 153
  ditto-ness, 157
  Evangeline, 150–152
  free interpretation, 155, 157
  metaphor, 151, 152, 156
  meter and poetic foot, 153–154
    anapestic foot, 154
    dactyllic foot, 154
    iambic foot, 153–154
    trochaic foot, 154
  meter types, 154
  Poems to Enjoy, 153
  "pyhrric," 154
  pyramiding, 158
  read assignments silently, 151
  Reflections on a Gift of Watermelon Pickle, 151, 153
  scansion, 154
  simile, 151, 152, 156
  simple approach, 151
  Song of Myself, 156–157, 158
  "spondaic," 154
  vocabulary, 124–125
    (*see also* Vocabulary)
  Whitman, 157, 158
  writing, 61–68
    (*see also* Writing)
Posture, oral composition, 89–90
Presentations, formal, 79–80

Productivity, creative:
  haiku poetry, 211–215
    buoyant voice, 213
    candor, 213
    deep affection, 215
    facetious voice, 214
    personification, 213–214
    philosopher, 214
    plaintive commentary, 212
    quiet outrage, 211–212
    romantic, 214–215
    simple observation, 212–213
  multi-paragraph composition, 190–199
  narrative with dialogue, 199–202
  poetry, 202–215
  single-paragraph composition, 181–190
Program, staggered-weekly-schedule, 30–32
Programmed Vocabulary, 120–121
Proofreading, 71
Prose, 125–126
Punctuation, dialogue, 54
"Pyhrric," 154
Pyramiding, 158

Q

Question mark, 55
Quizzes (*see* Tests)
Quotation marks, 54
Quotations, 54, 56, 57

R

Reading lab:
  average and above-average readers, 138, 145–146
  book-dividend system, 143, 145
  developmental reading, 141–142
    bibliographies, 142
    dual-level text, 141
    economical tool, 142
    fall reading test, 142
    low-ability students, 141
    patience and perceptiveness, 142
    preselection preparation, 141
    realistic approach, 142

Reading lab (*contd.*)
  developmental reading (*contd.*)
    recall through discussion, 141
    segmented readings, 141
    self-expression, 142
    speed, 141
    timed-silent-reading periods, 142
    workbook, 141–142
  discussion, 149–150
  dividend time, 143
  free reading, 164–165
  group reading, 146–149
    assignments for week, 146
    discussion period, 147–149
    number of groups, 146
    study guide questions, 147
    troublesome vocabulary, 147
  multiple-level, multiple-text, 143–145
    assignments, 144
    discussions, 145
    examples, 144
    length of segment, 143
    likes and dislikes, 145
    number of segments, 143
    recall and retention, 145
    "teacher's edition," 144
    teacher's questions, 145
    two or three levels, 145
  novel, 158–164
    per quarter, 160–164
    teaching, 158–160
  paperbacks, 137–140
    accumulating for library, 139
    attitude problems, 138
    book club, 138
    card-catalogue, 139
    class library, 138
    fascinate young readers, 137
    "in" and "out" system, 139
    increased reading, 138
    indispensable, 138
    partial basis for programs, 138
    personal developmental program, 138
    pleasure, 138, 139
    problem readers, 138
    student attitudes and skills, 140

Reading lab (contd.)
  paperbacks (contd.)
    variety, 139–140
    voluntary program, 138
  poetry survey, 150–158
    junior high school, 151–153
    senior high school, 153–158
  problem reader, 140–141
  "short burst" theory, 143
  summary, 165–167
Reflections on a Gift of Watermelon
    Pickle, 151, 153
Relocation, revision, 68, 70
Resource unit, oral composition, 84–88
Revision techniques, 68–71
  (see also Writing)

S

Scansion, 154
Schedule, staggered—weekly, 30–32
Scope, program, 18, 23
Sequence, 18
Sequential advancement, 53–54
Signalling, oral composition, 97
Similes, 151, 152, 156
Size of class, 19–20, 23, 29–31
Song of Myself, 156–157, 158
Speed talker, 92–93
"Spondaic," 154
Subject matter, delineation, 23
Summer institutes, 18
Syntax:
  base for exploration, 106–109
    (see also Grammar)
  writing, 49–50
    (see also Writing)

T

Talker, speed, 92–93
Tape recorder, 98–99
Teacher role:
  student-oriented discussion, 81
  writing, 71–75
    (see also Writing)
Teaching techniques, writing, 45–49
  (see also Writing)
Television, oral composition, 79

Testing:
  grammar, 113–116
  vocabulary, 124–130
Tests, 21, 23, 34–35
Texts, 23, 104–105
  (see also Grammar)
Today's Education, 115
Transformation, revision, 69, 70, 71
Trivia:
  grades, 21
  grammar drillwork, 20
  groups, 20–21
  language, 23
  nonacademic administrative, 21
  Oblivia, 22
  tests, 21
Trochaic foot, 154

U

Unity, 45

V

Vocabulary:
  dictionary use, 120
  drillwork, 133–134
    effectiveness, 133
    monotony and meaninglessness,
      133
    necessity, 133
    one test every six weeks, 134
    orally spell missed words, 133
    save and check, 133
    students who excel, 134
    weekly testing, 134
    written, 133
  inter-student correcting, 132–133
    constant hand-raising, 132
    time-saver, 132
    wrong decisions, 133
  lists of significant words, 120
  literature, 120
  period each week, 23
  programed learning approach, 120
  Programed Vocabulary, 120–121
    developed by James I. Brown, 121
    14 important roots, 121
    laboratory conditions, 121
    Lyons and Carnahan's, 120

Vocabulary (*contd.*)
  Programmed Vocabulary (*contd.*)
    mnemonics, 121
    reduced necessity for weekly test, 121
    student moves at own pace, 121
    20 important prefixes, 121
    workbook, 121
  summary, 135–136
  techniques, 122–123
    context of word, 123
    deskside visits, 123
    importance of vocabulary learning, 123
    isolation of itemization, 123
    literature and composition, 123
    pocket dictionary, 122
    troublesome words, 123
    without workbook, 122
  testing, 124–130
    commentary, 126
    correct word-meaning part, 127
    discussion technique, 127, 130
    flexibility, 129
    incorporate words in paragraph, 124
    inter-student correcting, 127
    italicized sentences, 128
    key word in topic sentence, 126–127
    option, 124
    oral approach, 128, 129
    poem, 124–125
    prose, 125–126
    spelling-only type, 124, 127
    troublesome words, 127
    types alternated, 124
    word meaning exercise, 127
    written spelling-meaning type, 124, 127
  word meaning, 121–122
  words can be fun, 130–132
  workbook, 119–122
    checking lessons, 122
    damage to English students, 120
    drill, end in itself, 119–120
    extra credit, 122
    inter-student collaboration, 120

Vocabulary (*contd.*)
  workbook (*contd.*)
    laboratory conditions, 120, 121, 122
    mandatory, 122
    not used advantageously, 119
    optional written work, 122
    ponderous and impractical, 120
    proper use, 119
    sequential structure, 119
    supervision, 120
    test scores, 120
    three periods a week, 120
    use required, 120
    year-end course evaluations, 134–135
Volume, oral composition, 95–96

W

Weekly program, 30–32
Workbooks, 119–122, 141–142
Work load, oversized classes, 19–20, 23
Writing:
  composition, 41–45
  dialogue, 54–58
    attributal break, 56
    attributive, 54, 55, 56, 57
    broken quotations, 56, 57
    chalkboard, 56–57
    comma value, 54, 55, 56
    conventional attributive, 54, 55, 56
    credible tone, 54, 57–58
    effects of primers, 58
    exclamation mark, 55
    indenting, 54, 57
    inferred attributive, 54, 55
    noun of address, 56
    period value, 55, 56
    punctuation, 54
    question mark, 55
    quotation marks, 54
    two-person, 56
  eclectic approach, 59–61
  multi-paragraph, 49, 58–59
  paragraph, 50–53
  poetry, 61–68
    adolescents, 65
    alliteration, 64

Writing (*contd.*)
  poetry (*contd.*)
    deskside visits, 64–65
    free verse, 65
    fundamentals, 64
    haiku, 66–68
    junior high, 61, 64
    literature phase, 61, 63, 64
    mechanics, 61
    new dimensions in forms, 64
    nuances and complexities, 63
    option of prose, 61, 63
    poetic license, 64
    student creations, 62
    suggesting alternatives, 65–66
    "survey," 61
    technical language, 61
    techniques of description, 64
    unit, 62
    visual and audio forms, 64
  revision techniques, 68–71
    addition, 69, 70
    elimination, 68, 70
    hypothetical paragraph, 69
    principle, 70
    proofreading, 71
    relocation, 68, 70
    transformation, 69, 70, 71

Writing (*contd.*)
  role of teacher, 71–75
    assigning compositions, 72–73
    enthusiasm, 71
    folders, 75
    gaining confidence, 72
    green markings, 74–75
    marking symbols, 74
    return creation next day, 73–74
    written comments, 74
  sequential advancement, 53–54
  summary, 75–77
  syntax, 49–50
  techniques, teaching, 45–49
    attractive style, 46
    continuity, 46
    description, 45–46, 47
    diction, 46
    exposition, 46–47
    grade levels, 48–49
    jotting down ideas, 48
    "on your own terms," 49
    persuasion, 46, 47
    program, 45
    single-paragraph development, 45–46, 48, 49
    unity, 45